Stepmothers

Stepmothers

Keeping It Together With Your Husband and His Kids

Merry Bloch Jones
and
Jo Ann Schiller

A BIRCH LANE PRESS BOOK
Published by Carol Publishing Group

A Birch Lane Press Book
Published by Carol Publishing Group
Birch Lane Press is a registered trademark of Carol
Communications, Inc.
Editorial Offices: 600 Madison Avenue, New York, N.Y. 10022
Sales & Distribution Offices: 120 Enterprise Avenue, Secaucus,
N.J. 07094
In Canada: Canadian Manda Group, P.O. Box 920, Station U,
  Toronto, Ontario M8Z 5P9
Queries regarding rights and permissions should be addressed to
Carol Publishing Group, 600 Madison Avenue, New York, N.Y. 10022

Carol Publishing Group books are available at special discounts
for bulk purchases, for sales promotions, fund raising, or
educational purposes. Special editions can be created to specifications.
For details, contact: Special Sales Department, Carol Publishing
Group, 120 Enterprise Avenue, Secaucus, N.J. 07094

Manufactured in the United States of America
10 9 8 7 6 5 4 3 2 1

Library of Congress Cataloging-in-Publication Data

Jones, Merry Bloch.
    Stepmothers : keeping it together with your husband and his kids /
Merry Bloch Jones and Jo Ann Schiller.
        p.   cm.
    ISBN 1–55972–120–0
    1. Stepmothers—United States.   2. Stepfamilies—United States.
I. Schiller, Jo Ann.   II. Title.
HQ759.92.J66   1992
306.874—dc20   92–11479
                                                         CIP

To our husbands, Robin and Berle,
without whom there would never have been
Morgan, Sarah, Jonathan, Joseph or Abby,
let alone Baille, Neely or Maggie.

And

To Herman S. Bloch,
who is so sorely missed.

Contents

Acknowledgments

This book could never have been written without the honesty, candor and willing participation of all of the stepmothers who shared their stories with us. We want to thank them for both their enthusiastic responses and their ongoing encouragement.

We'd also like to thank Hillel M. Black of Carol Publishing Group, for having confidence in our ideas and abilities, and Bruce Shostak, our editor at Birch Lane Press, for his thoroughness, thoughtfulness and sensitivity.

Additionally, we each have individuals we'd like to thank.

Merry wants to express heartfelt thanks to the members of her family who endured so much during the two years of this book's creation. Specifically, she wants to thank her husband, Robin, for his input on the law, his instructions on the computer, his help in cooking dinner on so many evenings so she could work, and his incredible, undying patience and diligence in reading, rereading and discussing the book as it progressed. She wants to thank her children, Baille and Neely, who sacrificed untold hours of "quality time" so that she could work without interruption, who always greeted her with elation when she'd take a break and who never seemed to bear a grudge. She thanks her mother, E. Judith Bloch, for having faith in her and for teaching her that any goal *can* be reached by taking just "one step at a time."

And, belatedly, she thanks her father, Herman S. Bloch, for inspiring his children to "do their best," for taking relish in the concept of this book and for expressing his joy in seeing her write. Finally, she wants to acknowledge her stepchildren, Morgan and Sarah, who, she hopes, will someday understand.

Jo Ann would like to thank her parents, Betty Lou and Leonard Malmud, and her sister Liz Rultenberg, for willingly and lovingly making themselves integral parts of her "family." She thanks her in-laws, Morris and Edith Schiller, who think they deserve no credit, but do, indeed. She wants to acknowledge her stepchildren, Jonathan, Joseph and Abby, who, whether they believe it or not, have a unique and special place in her heart. She thanks her daughter, Maggie, for her indestructible smile. And she wants to tell her husband, Berle, that he was right when he said, "Hang together or hang alone."

Introduction

I often wonder why, when I tell someone I'm a stepmother, I feel slightly ashamed, as if I'm revealing a dark family secret. Privately, I feel that I should get a *medal* for accepting the role. This contradiction isn't about whether I'm a good or a bad stepmother. It's about how it *feels* to be one.

—Maggie Joyner, Stepmother

We, the authors of this book, are stepmothers. We feel neither pride nor shame about this fact. We automatically assumed this title when we happened to marry men with children. For us, stepchildren were simply part of that package called "husband."

As we sat together at a kitchen table one day, we began to compare experiences. We were intrigued that, despite vast differences in our stepfamilies, there were so many similarities in our feelings about our roles. Although we were each sorry to hear about the other's difficulties, we were delighted to find a "soul mate." Neither of us, of course, could solve the other's problems, but we felt that the process of sharing thoughts and feelings with someone who truly understood lightened our loads.

During our conversation we discovered that each of us, independently, had wanted to write about stepmothers. The concept of a book was at first loosely defined and abstract. We knew only that there was a great deal to say and a great need to say it. With cups of decaf in hand, we talked ideas, theories and emotions. What emerged was a commitment to express stepmothers' stories in their own words. Our book would search for common ground and, where possible, present the wisdom of women who had acquired it firsthand. By the time we finished our danishes, the premise of our book was born.

Writing it took a little longer. Our lives were already full. Between us, we had three children and five stepchildren, ranging in age from six months to sixteen years. One of us was a graduate student in a master's program, working part-time as a management consultant; the other a writer and video producer with her own production company. Yet many of our obligations paled in light of our new project, which we attacked with vigor.

First, we needed to know whether other stepmothers would be interested in our project. We designed and sent surveys to friends who were stepmothers, to friends of friends who were stepmothers and to friends of friends of friends who were stepmothers. Later, we added others, referred to us by family physicians, therapists and attorneys. Our initial questionnaires sought to obtain demographic information and impressions of and experiences in stepmothering.

We thought that a response to our questionnaire of ten to twenty percent would be good. We were astounded to receive a return of almost ninety-five percent. Our surveys were returned to us not only filled-in, but with stream-of-consciousness outbursts that spilled into and all over the margins. Many of the stepmothers referred us to others who wanted to participate in the study. Armed with these new names, we sent out another round of surveys; they, too, came flying back.

The enthusiasm that greeted our surveys gave us the impetus and information we needed to continue. Stepmothers wrote us personal notes, thanking us for addressing issues that plagued them and praising us for our efforts. Since the response was so overwhelming, we decided to call the women who didn't answer the questionnaire to ask why. Our calls uncovered a remarkable depth of feeling. These women were so upset with their role that they were incapable of facing it long enough to spend the few minutes needed to answer our surveys.

Our initial surveys were followed by individual, in-depth interviews that lasted up to four hours. We talked with fifty-two women whose husbands have children from prior marriages that ended in divorce. Again, most of the women participated eagerly, offering more than the information we requested. The few women who opted to drop out of the study indicated that they had too much, rather than not enough, interest and involvement in our topic. One told us that her stepchildren were finally grown and out of her house and that she needed a break from them and her feelings about them. Another refused an interview because stepmothering was something she disliked, "just like if you work at a job you can't stand, the last thing you want to do is come home and talk about it for four hours." A third dropped out after she filed for divorce, blaming her stepdaughters for the breakup. Most, however, were so eager to participate that it was difficult to keep interviews down to four hours. At the beginning of our project, we had no inkling of the enthusiastic support these women would give us, the extent to which they would allow us to probe into their private lives or the profound way each one's story would touch us.

We did not intend that the group we interviewed would represent a random sample of all American stepmothers; we were not seeking to create the broadest definition of the "typical" stepmother. Rather, we wanted to provide a supportive, understanding voice to a large and growing group of women struggling with a role that usually receives little appreciation and has endured an abominable reputation through centuries of folklore and literature. Accordingly, based on their survey information, we selected a sample of women who are well-educated, sophisticated and accustomed to succeeding in relationships and life in general, so that any failures or difficulties they had at stepmothering would not be construed as characteristic. The women we spoke with are scattered across the country, from California to New York, Massachusetts to Florida. They are doctors and dentists, teachers and psychologists, advertising executives, attorneys and financial planners. For some, this was their first marriage. Others had been married before. Some had children of their own.

We held interviews in our homes, in their homes, in health clubs, parks, coffee shops and malls, always out of earshot of both stepchildren and husbands. Several women confided that their husbands had no idea how they truly felt about being stepmothers. Some feared that their husbands and, therefore, their marriages, could not withstand the exposure of these feelings. Despite such concerns, our participants spoke candidly and without reserve, requesting *only* that we disguise them and their stories in our book. Those requests attest to just how private and personal—no matter how universal—the plight of the stepmother is. We have been careful to assure anonymity; any resemblance between the composite characters used to illustrate our findings and actual people is purely coincidental.

Although none of our characters is intended to resemble an actual individual, each represents a definite type, or category, of response. They are composite characters, drawn from the collective experiences of the fifty-two women we interviewed and matching their profiles in terms of age, education, profession, socioeconomic status, spirits, outlooks and emotions.

As stepmothers, we have found confusion about family roles and relationships to be a significant and, at times, agonizing part of our lives. Our own experiences, in fact, have been so challenging that we were convinced there must be many other stepmothers and stepfamily members who needed to hear that there *is* hope. Granted, we *have* spoken to some stepmothers who say that they are completely happy in their roles and that they have no problems whatsoever with their stepfamilies. This book is not for or about these women: Where there are no problems, no solutions are needed.

Instead, this book concentrates on those stepmothers who *do* encounter difficulties and whose families, in most cases, manage their problems with, at best, mixed results. It shows how, even in painfully draining stepfamily situations, many stepmothers have found solutions, balances, internal coping mechanisms and compromises that work.

It is our hope that by sharing their experiences stepmothers will be able to help each other clarify their roles and ease some of their frustrations. We hope, too, that by reading what it's like to *be* a stepmother, stepchildren, their parents and others might broaden their understanding of the role.

Many of the women upon whom we based our book have become strong advocates of our effort to explore stepmothers' roles. Some see our success in completing this book as an affirmation of their success as stepmothers. Because they revealed their private experiences, they feel they have made personal investments in the well-being of stepfamilies everywhere. We hope that those who so eagerly took part in our project will share our pride in the fact that this book has become a reality. We thank them, hope that their contributions help others, and wish them each their own brand of success, as they choose it.

Stepmothers

ONE

Welcome to the Family

Ambush

"Now, for the first time ever, let us welcome Mr. and Mrs. Alex Slade!" Jennifer flushed at the announcement by the master of ceremonies, the applause of the guests, the music, the strong arm of her new husband sweeping her into her wedding reception.

Friends swarmed around the couple, and the groom was pulled away in conversation, leaving Jen with acquaintances she hardly knew. It was then she noticed a fairly steady tapping on her shoulder. She ignored it at first; no one was standing directly behind her. The thought of an annoying insect, a gnat perhaps, crossed her mind, but a gnat wouldn't be big enough to disturb her wedding veil, so she discounted it, and continued to chat with the Shermans (or was it the Sheldons?). Finally, a particularly heavy thwack thumped her veil. Reflex forced her to reach around and touch her shoulder.

Spitballs, gummy and soggy, clung to her wedding veil. A few had fallen to the floor and stickily lay close to her satin shoes. Stunned, Jennifer turned to see her new nine-year-old stepson, David, glaring at her. His eyes silently dared her to confront him as he defiantly reloaded his straw and took aim.

Servitude

"My fantasies about being a stepmother shattered the very day we married," sighed thirty-six-year-old pediatrician Julie Sinclair, whose husband has physical custody of his three children. Her fingers tightened around her coffee cup.

"We came home from our wedding at about 6:00 P.M., so we had a few hours to get ready for our midnight fight to Europe for our honeymoon. Some friends and my husband's three children came back to the house with us. I thought we'd have a few drinks, finish packing, relax together...

"Instead, I came home from my fantasy wedding to three kids who needed dinner. I hadn't anticipated my wedding ending with me cooking, cleaning and caring for three kids. My husband played football with them outside, like it was just a normal weekend evening. I stood watching them from the kitchen window."

Julie paused, looking out that same window, as if seeing not the snowy backyard, but the events that followed her wedding. After a moment, she turned and continued her story with a studied, controlled calm. "Intellectually, I knew Trevor needed to pay attention to the children, that they needed him. Emotionally, I couldn't stand it and realized I was glimpsing the rest of my life. Somewhere, right then, as I stood alone at the window, a small flicker ignited that, through the years, has turned into an intense raging fire. I don't know exactly what I'm raging at. I know it's not my husband, myself, or even the kids. But it's there, and, after five years, I'm still raging."

Becoming a Stepmother

Every day 1,300 new stepfamilies are formed in the United States. By the year 2000, one of every four children in this country will live with a stepparent by the age of sixteen, and more than half of all American families will be stepfamilies. For better or worse, the traditional concept of the "typical" family, with its clear-cut boundaries and mother, father, son and daughter roles, no longer applies.

Despite consistently high rates of divorce and remarriage over the last several decades, roles and relationships within blended, postdivorce families remain vague and ill-defined. More and more people find themselves in stepfamilies, but few know what to expect from each other, or even from themselves, in this context.

Cracking the Ice

We began our investigation of these relationships by asking each woman to describe when she first considered herself a stepmother. Was it at her wedding, before marriage, or during some poignant event shared with the children? We learned, however, not *when* the role became real to her, but *how*, and we were surprised that almost all of the women responded with upsetting, even traumatic experiences. The stories of the stepmothers we've called Jennifer Slade and Julie Sinclair tell of trouble that began on their wedding days, but each represents a different type of experience. Jennifer is one of many women whose first memories of being stepmothers consist of facing unexpected hostility from their stepchildren. Julie is like many others whose first memories are of being overwhelmed by the realization that their stepchildren's needs will forever compete with, and usually take precedence over, their own.

For many other women, the first memory of being stepmothers is of being flatly rejected by their stepchildren. Unaccustomed to rejection, they refuse to accept the children's response and embark upon personal crusades to win them over. Molly Jerome, a forty-two-year-old special education teacher, shuddered as she remembered her stepsons' initial reactions to her.

"I first realized what I as in for as a stepmother at my stepson Brian's eighth birthday party," she recalls. "He looked from his cake to me and declared, 'I hope you die,' before he blew out the candles. Seriously! And when he learned that our wedding was going to be held at my mom's, he told us he wished her house would burn down. I'll never forget it."

Many women say that their stepchildren don't start out voicing hostilities or rejection. In fact, many emphasize that verbalized, open expressions of anger give them an ironic sense of accomplishment. "At least," Molly explains, "when he wished me dead, he was *talking* to me. In the beginning of my relationship with Ed, his kids shut me out altogether. I was shocked—I'd never met people who absolutely did not want to know me! Maybe they thought that if they ignored me, I'd go away. They were icy and silent. Ed became so upset and tense that he couldn't talk. So, for a long time, whenever I was around my stepchildren, *I* was the only one I could have a conversation with, and I did. I jabbered on and on to fill the silence...."

For Molly, as for many stepmothers, the initial challenge was to make her stepchildren perceive her as an individual, rather than as an interloper in their broken family. Women like Molly believe that the first step in being accepted by their stepchildren is for the children to release their anger and express their feelings, however negative. Their stepchildren, though, are often "polite" or "well brought up," and are thus uncomfortable expressing anger at adults. Because they don't know how to communicate anger "acceptably" they often express it indirectly, through silence or resistant behavior.

Stepmothers who face such rejection often find that it takes a lot of time, patience and consistency to get their stepchildren to relax enough to express themselves. Despite years of effort, some never gain acceptance by their stepchildren. However, most women who persist in being warm, nonthreatening and nonjudgmental eventually penetrate the barriers and form foundations for relationships.

"I had to remain affectionate and friendly *all* the time," Molly remembers. "I had to be calm, entertaining and sweet, even when they'd refuse to greet me or to help me carry the tons of groceries I bought for them. My efforts finally paid off, though. It took months, but I succeeded. I got through to them. My stepsons actually relaxed enough to tell me and Ed quite explicitly how they felt about having me in their lives. I didn't *like* what they said, but I could hardly complain, because they were letting us in on their feelings. And that was when I first knew I was a stepmother—when they began to *say* how angry they were, how they hated me and even wished I were dead. It hurt, but I knew that we were getting somewhere and that we could help them, now that they were opening up."

Captive Audience

While some stepmothers have difficulty getting stepchildren to express themselves, others cannot get them to stop. Their stepchildren communicate so openly, and depend on them so heavily that they feel unprepared and inadequate. Some of these stepchildren are hungry for attention or limits; others are looking for assurances that their stepmothers will put up with them, no matter how wild they get. A few are acting out a general rage about their parents' divorces and their confusion about family relationships.

Maggie Joyner, a thirty-nine-year-old psychiatric nurse, recalls worrying about her responsibilities as a stepmother, almost from the day she met her teenage stepson. "The first clue I had that being a stepmother to Josh was going to be...challenging was when his dad took us out to dinner to get acquainted and he started to behave in, well, inappropriate ways." Maggie pauses, smiles and shrugs. "See, Josh is a karate expert and he got up and began practicing his karate right in the restaurant. Right next to the dessert cart. Then, as we left, he leapt over cars in the street outside the restaurant, alarming drivers and passersby."

Women in situations like Maggie's say that their first memories of being stepmothers are of seeing their stepchildren do virtually anything to get attention, including potentially dangerous and destructive activities. They recall being tested and feeling that their stepchildren were begging them to take on responsibility, create structure in their lives and set limits, even before they had established their roles and relationships as stepmothers. Many still struggle to define their roles and the scope of their responsibilities. They often blame their stepchildren's parents for being lenient or even neglectful in their roles as parents. Some, like Maggie, think that the parents, guilt-ridden over their divorces, try to compensate and express their love for their children by avoiding discipline or rules.

"That first night," Maggie remembers, "I realized that, by default, limit-setting was going to fall to me. But I didn't feel I had any *authority* to set limits for Josh. I stood there, watching him fling himself over automobiles and thought, 'Oh boy.' And I knew, while he was still in the air, while his dad was acting like this was normal or not happening, that this was both very *much* happening and not at *all* normal. While strangers gaped at us, I had this ominous, gut feeling that the worst was yet to come, and that feeling still hasn't gone away."

Caught in the Crossfire

Many women recall their initial experiences as stepmothers as conflicts with their stepchildren's mothers. Some described stepchildren as pawns in the ongoing battles between divorced parents. As newcomers, stepmothers become easy targets of the pawns. Although many stepmothers expected that there would be conflicts between ex-spouses, most were unprepared for the intensity of the anger aimed at *them* by their stepchildren's mothers.

"When I was introduced to my stepchildren, they were polite little soldiers, ages four and eight. A perfect little girl and boy," recalls Mia Jordan, a thirty-six-year-old artist. "I had no idea that there was more to it than that until bathtime the first night they spent with us. Their mother had packed towels and sheets for them. I said that that wasn't necessary, since we had plenty of extras. But they said their mother had forbidden them to use my linens because, if they did, they'd get a disease. They were genuinely scared, because, when their dad insisted that this was ridiculous, they both dissolved into tears, crying for their mother. I was so insulted I was shaking. It ended in a marathon phone confrontation with their mother, Kate, who ranted in anger about my husband, about me, about her children's visits with us and, oh yes, about what she wished would happen to us both—real soon. At the end of that phone call, there were two red-eyed, exhausted children who fell asleep too tired to bathe anyway. I suppose all of Kate's pent-up emotion had to come out, somewhere, but it was so sad. The kids felt only the pain. They were in the middle of dangerous territory, caught between adults they loved. They were the victims of pretty fierce emotions. But *their* reactions to what was going on weren't being addressed. It was scary. I'd never even met their mother. I'd only recently met *them*. And, because I loved their father, I was suddenly drawn into an old war. I and my linens had become the focus of decades of bitter frustration."

Stepmothers like Mia, finding themselves under attack, are forced to defend themselves even though they are outsiders in the fight between ex-spouses. Some of them become heavily involved, side with their husbands and attempt to counter the ex-wives' accusations and win their stepchildren's favor. The majority, however, eventually find the battles exhausting and simply not theirs to fight.

"At the time of the incident with the sheets," Mia remembers, "I had no hesitation, no doubt about where I stood. I was indignant and righteous, and I took a stand. But, as time passed, I dropped out. I don't want to be a target or to use all my energy in combat. It's not my place. I have no stake in their disputes. But it took me years to figure that out."

Many stepmothers remember their introductions to the role as intense displays of anger, whether icy silence, auto-leaping antics, symbolic spitballs or shunned sheets. The source of the anger may be the stepchildren, their mothers or someone else, but the one constant is that most stepmothers who are targeted, even those who are prepared intellectually for the impact of divorce on children and former spouses, are stunned by the emotional effects of having the residual rages, frustrations and hurts of their husbands' former families aimed at them.

Other stepmothers are shocked not by the anger that *greets* them in their new families, but by their *own* anger, when they realize, as Julie did, how their new roles promise to alter their lives in ways they had never anticipated.

Changing Diapers, Changing the Family

Although anger is the dominant theme in most stepmothers' early memories, many women have no significant memories of being stepmothers until after they've become biological mothers as well. For them, the birth of children precipitated conflicts with their stepchildren, with the mothers of the stepchildren and even with their husbands, the fathers of the new arrivals.

Marla Jenson, a thirty-five-year-old banking executive, said her first experiences of stepmotherhood consisted of a series of explosions. "The big bomb fell four months after our wedding, when I told my stepchildren I was pregnant. They were teenagers, so I had assumed they could handle it. But, after I told them, my stepson, Eric, looked disgusted and sneered, 'I can't believe you're doing this at *your* age.' Tiffany, who was eighteen, stood up dramatically and cried, 'I'm telling you up front: if it's a girl, I'll hate her forever!' and ran out of the room.

"My husband, Steve, ran after her, to comfort her. He later blamed *me* for upsetting them by 'not preparing' them before I told them. When they told their mother about the baby, she became wildly jealous and took my husband back to court, to sue for more support, saying that, since there was going to be a new baby, she was worried about the future monies my husband would give *her* children. Everyone was angry. It got so bad that I wished, for a while, that I hadn't married

Steve, even though I loved him dearly and desperately wanted our baby."

The introduction of new babies into blended families like Marla's releases hidden tensions and latent hostilities. The structures of their stepfamilies are so delicate, their relationships so tenuous, that the very *idea* of a new player, even a small one, sets the entire family off balance. Sometimes the pregnancy becomes a catalyst for the family's members to express their feelings, opening the way for solutions. But, because it seems to cement the stepmother's marriage, it often precipitates deeper trouble. The new arrivals can initiate rivalries that force their fathers into repeatedly choosing between wife and ex-wife and between the competing needs of half-siblings.

Marla remembers a vivid mental picture that appeared to her as her husband chased Tiffany out of the door. She imagined herself holding a screaming baby, while Steve, his ex-wife and his children all grappled with each other, grabbing, clawing and refusing to let go. Although fleeting, the image was powerful, and, in retrospect, she says it was accurate. "They've kept on beating at Steve," she remarks, "whether through the courts, his wallet or his heartstrings."

His Baby, Her Baby

Like Marla, many women do not take much notice of being stepmothers until they have their own children. Often, the resulting rivalries pull their husbands apart. Others, however, say that they themselves become the focus of competition. Their stepchildren vie with their biological children for attention; their own children can be jealous of half-siblings when they visit. A few women say that their husbands' ex-wives are so jealous that they try to involve themselves in the new babies' lives. Of all the rivalries stepmothers describe, however, perhaps the most troubling are those generated by their husbands.

Some stepmothers find that the birth of their babies causes a division between them and their husbands that threatens the structure of their families and even their marriages. Maxine James, a thirty-three-year-old dentist, explains: "My stepdaughter visits every weekend. It *was* fun. But everything changed when our baby, Ruth, was born. Gordon, my husband, was wonderful during the birth. He was right there with me, very loving and attentive. I thought that we'd reached a new level of intimacy. But, the night before I was to leave the hospital, Gordon seemed to be a different person. His only concern was for his daughter, Tina. He wanted her to hold the baby, to be with us when we took the baby home, to stay with us for the first few nights and generally to be the center of attention, so she wouldn't feel left out. I felt as if Gordon had punched me, as if he'd forgotten all about me. My nipples hurt, I had a fever, my episiotomy ached. I wanted to hold his hand, nurse my baby and sleep, *not* entertain my stepdaughter. I got hysterical."

Maxine remembers her rage at being pulled away from her *own* child in order to accommodate her stepchild. "When he saw how upset I was," Maxine recalls, "Gordon explained, quite rationally, that the new baby wouldn't know what was going on, but seven-year-old Tina *would*, and that she'd have adjustment problems that would require special attention. I could follow his reasoning, but his forcing Tina into my life at that moment robbed me of something that was precious and irreplaceable. I needed to have some time to put my own little family together before dealing with her. It's almost four years later, and, when I talk about it, I'm still upset. My feelings and my anger at being pulled and pressured have never been addressed."

Most women in situations like Maxine's are genuinely fond of their stepchildren and want to have close relationships with them. But when they have their own children, they discover fundamental differences between their own and their husbands' definitions of family. They define their families as spouses, children and stepchildren; their husbands define them as spouses and children, without differentiation. These stepmothers want to define separate relationships with their stepchildren; their husbands want equal status for all the children.

"The reason we fight is always the same," Maxine sighs. "I see our family as three people; Gordon sees it as four. I stutter when people ask me how many kids I have because Gordon wants me to say two, but I know *I* only have one. I try to be as affectionate toward Tina as I was before Ruthie was born. But the pressure my husband puts on me makes me feel forced and unnatural."

Too Many Hats

For some women, motherhood changed the way they saw their roles as stepmothers.

"Until I had a child of my own, I had no problem with being a stepmother," says Jill Sterling, a thirty-nine-year-old advertising executive. "I had an intense need to nurture, and I gave my stepson all the attention and affection he could possible want. His visits completely centered on him. Camping, the ocean, horseback-riding lessons. I'd always try to surprise him with something, to win his affection.

"But when my first baby was born, I just couldn't do it anymore. And, I admit, I didn't want to. I can see that he resented the change; that, suddenly, a lot of energy was going elsewhere. At times, I actually felt indifferent to him. The contrast was shocking, even to me."

Most of these women were upset by how their feelings for their stepchildren changed after they had their own children. Many attributed the changes to maternal bonding and the emotional and physical exhaustion that can follow childbirth. Some tried to compensate by paying extra attention to their stepchildren, but found it difficult to focus on anything but their new babies.

"I'm sure it was tough for Charlie," Jill muses. "When he visited, I no longer cooked just for him or ran around to entertain him. I had diapers to change and a baby to feed, and I was tired. The bottom line is, I didn't want to concentrate on him as intensely anymore."

As their own children grow and demand more of them, many stepmothers find that the time they are willing to devote to their stepchildren diminishes. Jill explains, "I care about my stepson. But I don't want to get back into the pattern I was in, of personally trying to provide everything that he needs or wants. At one time, I tried to do everything for him, so he'd accept and love me. Now, I don't need that acceptance, and, as a mother myself, I'm more sensitive about the job of mothering. I realize that my stepson has his *own* parents. It's neither my place nor my desire to be a mother to him. It's not my job."

Along with diapers and 2:00 A.M. feedings, motherhood brings other changes to stepmotherhood. It unleashes jealousy from their husbands' ex-wives and rivalry from their stepchildren. It creates profound conflicts with husbands and raises fundamental questions about the definition of family. Emotional priorities, too, change with the arrival of babies. The need to nurture finds new outlets and many new mothers feel unable to participate in their step-relationships as intensely as before. More often, the new role of "mother" clarifies the differences between their responsibilities as "mothers" and as "stepmothers," and women describe their previous intensity with their stepchildren as misguided, saying their own needs, rather than the children's, dominated. "I needed to feel love for a child," confided one, "more than she needed the love of another adult. She already had two parents. It was what *I* needed that drove me." Many of these stepmothers eventually developed clear ideas of what limits they wanted on their relationships with stepchildren; however, a few lament that the children want or need more than they can give.

Sabotage

A number of women confessed that their first notable experiences as stepmothers involved marital problems, some of which were deliberately instigated by their stepchildren. One stepdaughter repeatedly created situations from which her father had to "rescue" her, playing on his guilt and love in order to woo him away from his new wife. Another created an intricate pattern of lies to befuddle her stepmother, to make it seem that her father was still seeing his ex-wife romantically. Not all of these situations were manageable. After just thirteen months of marriage, one stepmother filed for divorce, saying, "I just can't fight my stepchildren anymore. They've been out to get me since day one. My husband doesn't believe what I say anymore. He believes their lies. They got me. They win."

When stepchildren set out to sabotage their stepmother and destroy the marriage, its survival depends on the ability of the couple to identify the situation, communicate openly about it and present a united front. In some cases, though, it is not the stepchildren alone, but their father who actually draws the battlelines that ostracize the stepmother. When this happens, she has to rely on her own will and ingenuity, if she wants to remain in the family.

Jamie Simpkins, a forty-year-old attorney, recalls her first stepmother memory as a contest with her stepdaughter for her husband's attentions. "The summer after we married, we went to the mountains. It was supposed to be a belated honeymoon. I pictured a romantic, intimate escape from civilization, phones and responsibilities. Time for each other and nature and so on.

"But what happened was that Keith asked his six-year-old daughter, Brittany, to go with us. It was a disaster. I had to compete with a six-year-old for my husband's attention. Brittany was tired, so we couldn't hike. Brittany didn't like the beach, so we couldn't swim. Brittany thought the bait was 'disgusting,' so we couldn't fish. And, the corker, Brittany was afraid of the dark, so she had to sleep with us. I don't mean just with us in our room. I mean *with* us, *between* us, *in* our bed."

Women in situations like this describe themselves as the "third party in a relationship of two," as "intruders" or as "interlopers." They say they find it uncomfortable to participate in family activities because their husbands and their stepchildren relate to each other so intensely and exclusively. They find it impossible to resolve their problems because their husbands are unwilling or unable to tolerate criticism of their children.

"When Brittany came on our camping trip," Jamie recalls, "I found out what I was in for. The trip was *hers.* Just as the house was *hers* and the man in it was *her* father, not necessarily *my* husband. Life centered around *her.* I never saw things that way before our trip to the mountains. I've never seen them another way since."

Stepgranny

An account of the initiations into stepmothering would not be complete without recollections from women who are married to men with adult children. Most of these women say that whatever problems they had with their stepchildren when they were younger have continued into adulthood. However, some have become fast friends with their adult stepchildren, laughing about and lamenting the problems of earlier years. One says that her stepdaughter has recently married a man with children. "Oh, it's wonderful poetic justice," the stepmother laughs. "Sara calls me up screaming about her 'monster' stepsons, asking how I ever put up with her and her brother. Now, *she* knows what it means to be a stepmother!"

Some women sought to avoid the role of stepmother by waiting to marry until their husbands' children were grown. They were afraid their stepchildren would be divisive in their marriages. Jessie Solomon, a forty-two-year-old speech therapist, explains, "I knew long before I met my husband that I didn't want to marry anyone with children. When a man has kids with someone, part of him always belongs to the kids and their mother. I wanted no part of that. I wanted my husband to be *my* husband. I wanted my first child to be *his* first child. I didn't want to share *our* life with people from prior relationships."

These women describe themselves as romantic, idealistic, jealous, possessive and insecure. They admit that, no matter how long they delayed the wedding, the title "Mrs." brought with it the title of "Stepmother." Jessie remembers when she first realized that fact. "I thought Mark's kids were gone. That's the only reason I married him. I waited twelve years, until they'd all grown up and moved away! We had a son of our own. We were quiet and happy. But, just after our son was born, Mark's older daughter had a baby boy. Mark was suddenly a *grandfather*! All the long-lost relatives, friends and children—even Mark's ex-wife—reappeared to make a fuss over the grandchild, not over *our* son. Now, they all expect Mark to do grandfather things, which is great for *him*, but it just simply doesn't involve *me* at all. It makes our child seem unimportant."

To their dismay, whether stepmothers like it or not, fight it or accept it, participate or hide, they are still stepmothers, even step-grandmothers. Whether their stepchildren are fifteen or fifty, they are still stepchildren. the existence of these roles and relationships is not a matter of choice; the only options stepmothers and stepchildren have are how they handle them.

When describing their first memories of being stepmothers, women recounted an array of upset and upheaval. There are women who remember being absolutely baffled by the conflicting relationships and emotions into which they had stumbled by marrying men with children. There are others who felt competent, involved and comfortable as stepmothers, until they were overwhelmed by the all-consuming role of mother. Still others remember encountering unexpected vulnerabilities in their husbands, weaknesses in their marriages or limits in their own emotional capacities. Very few women present warm, peaceful accounts of being stepmothers.

As one stepmother remarked, "Cinderella may not have been treated all that well, but her stepmother may have had a point, too."

Two

Expectations

When they first marry, most brides are aglow with anticipation of love, romance and family. When her new husband has children from a prior marriage, however, a bride's expectations must expand to include images of her relationships with her stepchildren. The clearer these images are, the greater the chance that they will have to be redefined sometime after the wedding; the higher the expectations, the more likely they are to lead to disappointment. Conversely, stepmothers who expect little, who remain open-minded and flexible about their stepchildren and who allow relationships to develop at their own pace and along their own lines are the most likely to find satisfaction in their roles.

When they become stepmothers, most women have positive expectations: they anticipate happy families in which they will unite with their husbands as parental teams. Many use words like "supermom" or even "savior" to describe the person they expected to be for their stepchildren. Most expect to love their stepchildren and to be respected, accepted and loved by them in return.

Of the women we interviewed, only about one in ten had no expectations, either because their stepchildren were adults living on their own, or because they had absolutely no idea what the role would involve.

About a third of the stepmothers we spoke with reported negative expectations. They were concerned about their abilities to meet the needs and win the affection of their stepchildren. They worried about interfering with the relationships between their husbands and their stepchildren, and about the impact their stepchildren would have on their marriages. Those who brought children of their own to their marriages were often concerned about the relationships between their own children and their stepchildren and about avoiding favoritism and rivalries.

Regardless of their expectations, the majority find that their actual experiences as stepmothers are worse than they expected. Although years may have passed, many remain "outsiders" to the relationships between their stepchildren and their husbands; others feel "invisible" or "used." Some say that their stepchildren feel conflicted about liking them, as if, by doing so, they would betray their mothers. Many feel "invaded" by their stepchildren during visits; they talk of losing all privacy or becoming "servants" in their own homes.

About one fourth, however, find stepmothering a better experience than they expected. Some are surprised that they "fell in love" with their husbands' children. A few say that it is a lot of work, but worth it, because their stepchildren are vital to their husbands' happiness.

The initial attitudes and expectations of stepmothers rarely resemble the eventual reality of their relationships. Some women who expected to find big happy families did; others were disappointed. Some who expected dismal domestic situations were pleasantly surprised. Women whose stepchildren are adults were just as unable to predict their experiences as those who have young stepchildren. Women who have been married before, or who have children of their own, or who are over forty were just as baffled about what to expect as others. Women whose stepchildren live with them found their expectations to have been just as in, or out of, line with reality as those of women whose stepchildren visit only occasionally.

The patterns that do emerge are not in the *accuracy* of stepmothers' expectations, but in their *types*. First, there are those who expect to save their stepchildren from all harm, to perform perfectly and to satisfy everyone's needs. Next are those who expect to be part of happy, loving families and to form friendships with their stepchildren. Others expect their roles to bring them closer to their husbands, working together as unified parenting teams. A few expect that the role of stepmother will be isolating and divisive to their marriages. And some stepmothers have no idea what to expect, other than that they will have to be flexible and "roll with the punches."

Stepmoms and Superheroes

Some particularly ambitious stepmothers expect to "rescue" or "save" their stepchildren. They see them as victims of "raw deals" that resulted from their parents' unhappy marriages and divorces. They expect to be welcomed into their stepchildren's lives as the allies they intend to be. As newcomers, they expect that their stepchildren will not associate them with unhappy times and that they will be able to begin their relationships with clean slates.

These women see their stepchildren as "troubled," "angry" or even as "borderline juvenile delinquents" and feel uniquely challenged to come to their rescue. Some believe that they alone understand their stepchildren and can solve problems that baffled the parents. Others freely admit to a competitive desire to succeed where their stepchildren's mothers and fathers have failed. A few simply feel driven to be "a whopping success" as stepmothers and as new wives. Whatever their motives, most find that reality falls far short of their expectations.

Maggie Joyner describes her initial expectations as naive. Her stepson, Josh, was fifteen years old when she married his father, four years ago. Josh's mother insisted that Josh live with them.

"When Josh moved in, I intended to prove that all he needed was understanding, patience and someone to listen to him. I knew he'd been smoking dope and cutting school, but I thought that that was just because his parents had neglected him because of their *own* problems. *I*, on the other hand, was going to be sensitive to his needs. I had no idea what his presence would mean to *my* personal life, or how unprepared I was to deal with him. When I came home from work, wanting to soak in the tube and relax, I'd find Josh, stoned, listening to my stereo full blast. Breakfast and lunch dishes and scraps of food would be everywhere. I could tell he hadn't gone to school because he was still wearing what he had slept in the night before. Or, he'd practice his karate in my living room. He'd just bounce up and start 'karateing.'

"I never knew what to expect when I walked in the door. It got so bad that, rather than *saving* him, I couldn't stand *looking* at him. I hated coming home to my own house because Josh was everywhere I turned. I wasn't his parent and didn't want to be, yet his dad was working and his mom wouldn't have him, so who else was there to look after him?"

Many women like Maggie find that they have to lower their sights. Their intended "rescues" are stifled by growing resentment; their plans to "save" are ruined by feelings of suffocation. Most of them experience tremendous guilt about their negative feelings as well as about their failure to fix their stepchildren's problems. Many do not discuss their feelings with their husbands because their husbands are already distressed by their children's problems.

Stepmothers in this situation worry that they have failed their stepchildren, even though they feel crowded and exhausted by them. They say they don't want to become "just another adult who has let them down," or that "despite the problems *I'm* having, I still want to help *them.*" But, more than anything else, they express confusion. "I don't know," one stepmother said, "what I *should* be doing, what my responsibilities are. What *is* the job of a stepmother anyway?"

Like Maggie, most of these stepmothers never manage to "save" their stepchildren. Their failures may be due both to the depth of the stepchildren's problems and to the stepmothers' own doubts about their roles. However, when asked why she thinks her expectations weren't met, Maggie presents another theory: "The biggest reason I couldn't help Josh is that I allowed a situation to develop where there was no room in my life for myself. Josh's needs and my husband's needs were all I thought about. No one, especially me, looked out for what *I* needed. I guess I learned that you can't give effectively to others if you neglect yourself."

Everything to Everybody

Where stepmothers like Maggie expect to solve all their stepchildren's problems, others have even loftier expectations. A few intend to meet all the needs all the time of everyone in the family, including themselves. They dub themselves "perfect, professional wondermoms," "saint stepmothers" and "supermoms."

These women see themselves as powerful, efficient and in control of their lives. When they take on the role of stepmother, they expect that they will succeed as they have with everything else they have attempted. Pediatrician Julie Sinclair was thirty-one when she married into a ready-made family and accepted custody of Zack, eleven, Kevin, ten, and Tori, eight. "I expected that being a stepmother would be demanding, but I've always thrived on and enjoyed demanding roles. I had a clear-eyed vision of myself as superwoman: the perfect wife, stepmother, daughter, doctor, community leader and, eventually, mother. Simple. No problem." She chuckles, shakes her head and describes how reality measured up to her expectations.

"The first week of our marriage was chaos. Pure chaos. Trevor and I rushed home from work to slap dinner on the table, throw food down our throats and run around with rags and sponges cleaning up. Our evenings were consumed with homework, baths, laundry and bedtime stories. There were bouts of children yelling and crying. As newlyweds, Trevor and I directed all our energy not toward ourselves and our newfound wedded bliss, but toward meeting the needs of three kids."

Like others with expectations of personal perfection, Julie accepted the challenges of stepmothering without either hesitation or much thought about what the role would entail. After a while, she realized that she had taken on more than she had bargained for. "Sometime in the second or third week," Julie recalls, "it hit me that what I was doing was forever. It sunk in that the loads of laundry and piles of ironing would not get any smaller as the kids got older. I was stunned to realize that I would endlessly be doing for somebody else's kids the things I hated to do even for *myself.*"

Stepmothers like Julie are often bewildered by unfamiliar feelings of anger, indignation and panic that typically accompany the shock of the realities of their new role. Most, accustomed to overcoming obstacles, flatly refuse to accept defeat or even to admit that the challenges of being a stepmother are more than they are prepared to handle. "My initial expectations turned out to be accurate," one stepmother says. "I'd envisioned myself as superwoman, and that's who I became. I just hadn't envisioned that I'd hate being superwoman."

Despite their feelings, these women persevere, striving singlehandedly to meet the needs of everyone in the family. Some explain that, at their worst times, they find external motivations. "I *loved* people telling me what a saint I was and what a great job I was doing," one confided.

Another said that she wanted to prove to her family that she had *not* been wrong to marry a man with children. "My parents had been adamantly against the marriage, so I wanted to show them it was no problem. A snap!"

Finally, some of these high achievers are driven to prove that *they* can raise their stepchildren better than the natural mothers could. "I wanted Trevor to see me as a better parent than his ex-wife had been," Julie concedes. "And I didn't want anyone to see that I was the slightest bit unhappy, or making unwilling sacrifices, or that there were cracks in my armor."

Many stepmothers express dismay that their stepchildren seem oblivious to their efforts to please them. "No one ever said 'thank you,'" Julie remarks. "None of the kids seemed to take note of or appreciate what I was doing. Just one month earlier, I'd been single, responsible for no one but myself. I could eat an English muffin and a Coke for dinner at 2:00 A.M., if I wanted.

"Suddenly, I was cooking a well-balanced, planned and scheduled dinner for five people every night. This was a capital M *major* effort for me. When I complained to Trevor about his kids' lack of appreciation, he said that I was expecting too much, that his kids had a *right* to beds, a warm house and three meals a day. It struck me that he was right. I'd never thanked *my* parents for feeding *me*—why should *Trevor's* kids have to thank *us?* Since that revelation, appreciation hasn't been an issue for me. I don't expect it, so, on the rare occasions that I *do* hear it, it means even more."

Julie may have resolved the problem for herself, but many others find their pique at not being appreciated or thanked for their efforts builds over time. They agree that children have a right to expect "a bed and three meals a day" from their *parents*, but a number of stepmothers feel that they deserve some credit for providing for children when they are not their parents. While their husbands' appreciation and their own sense of accomplishment provide step-mothers like Julie with sufficient thanks, many others, especially among those who are supermoms, confess that they resent being taken for granted by their stepchildren. These women, who generally rely on positive feedback as a motivator, often find the role of stepmother almost unbearably thankless. Nevertheless, some stepmothers find that the issue of appreciation fades in importance as the children get older.

"With time," one explained, "the kids have become more self-sufficient. They don't need as much from me, so my job's easier. Plus, we've learned what we can expect from each other, they from me and me from them. As we stumbled along, somehow, somewhere, we became a family. Unlike other families, perhaps. But a family."

Stepmonster

On the other end of the stepmother spectrum from the supermoms are women who simply wish that their stepchildren would "disappear." These women so thoroughly despise having stepchildren that they have to hide their feelings from their husbands, creating invisible emotional barriers in their marriages. They recognize that their problems lie within themselves, and they are usually ashamed of their feelings. Most freely admit that, objectively, their stepchildren are decent people who make no unnecessary demands on their daily lives.

Jessie Solomon, forty-two, has two adult stepchildren, Todd, twenty-three, and Tricia, twenty-six. Jessie has nothing against her stepchildren as individuals. "If I'd met them someplace else, in another context, I might even like them," she sighs. "But, because they *are* my stepchildren, my stomach literally turns when their names are mentioned. I hate it that Mark's a grandfather when I'm not a grandmother. I hate it when his kids send him pictures of their families. I feel almost as jealous as I would if Mark were having an affair."

Jessie and others like her represent an emotional extreme. Although these women fully understand and easily articulate the irrational nature of their feelings, they have no interest in changing them. "I know I sound grotesque," one says. "I'm the stereotype, the wicked, evil stepmother. But, if I'm going to be honest, I have to say that I hate, loathe and despise my stepchildren, even though they've never done anything wrong. They are the dark side, the negative aspect of the total way I love my husband. They're a living symbol of a division between me and the man I love. They bring out the worst in me, the jealous, possessive, clutching part."

Ironically, the fact that these stepmothers refuse to relate to their stepchildren excludes them from large parts of their husbands' lives. By wanting *all* of their husbands' love and attention, they prevent themselves from participating in some of their husbands' most important relationships and, in so doing, defeat their own purpose.

"I *expected* it to get better, since they'd grown up and were living in their own homes," Jessie says. "But now I know it won't *ever* get better. As long as he loves them, as long as they exist, it won't change. It can't."

Fairy Godmother

If stepmothers who expect to hate their stepchildren represent one extreme, stepmothers who expect to accept them completely represent another. Many women simply assume that their stepmothering relationships will resemble other rewarding relationships they have had with children. They expect that their stepchildren will want to know, like and be liked by them.

Molly Jerome's stepsons were eight and nine years old when she married their father, five years ago. "I didn't know what the relationship would be or how we'd all end up feeling about each other," she remembers, "but I thought we'd all be in it together and that we'd work at it, to find out what was ahead for us as a family.

"Well...let's say my expectations were a bit off. My stepsons, Brian and Scott, absolutely did *not* want to get to know me. They made that clear, right from the start. They wanted their world to remain as it had been when their parents were together. They wanted nothing and no one to rock their boats."

Like Molly, many stepmothers are greeted by their stepchildren's anger, rather than their interest. Most of the hostilities are acted out, rather than spoken. "They'd leave messes for me to clean up," Molly says. "They'd throw their laundry into the hall, rather than into the hamper. They'd leave trash or dirty dishes lying around. They'd blitz the bathrooms. It sounds like small stuff, but it was out of hand. They treated me as their servant."

Stepmothers like Molly feel it is *their* responsibility to make their relationships with their stepchildren succeed. Accustomed to satisfying relationships with children, they feel frustrated and even at fault when they encounter difficulties with their stepchildren. Many attempt to decode messages in their stepchildren's behavior. Some read belligerence as a symbolic request for adult authority or limits.

Molly believed that, before she could begin to have a positive relationship with her stepchildren, she needed to establish a balance between affection and authority. "The limits I wanted to set followed a simple rule: it was okay for them to dislike me or to be upset with me, but they could *not* leave messes all around my house or be rude to me."

Women in Molly's position, however, find it difficult to establish limits and rules. They know they have to be consistent, establish patterns and stick with them. Molly remembers how she labored over her strategy. "I actually made a list of different approaches I could take, like weekly gripe sessions, or charts with chores. Finally, I decided I'd leave a note on their bedroom door that said, 'Clean up your room. Signed, your dirty-rotten-no-good-but-loving-stepmother.'

"It worked! They actually cleaned their room! The next time they visited, though, they threw their laundry into the hall, as usual. So, encouraged by my last victory, I bought them a bright red duffle bag, and left it in the corner of their room with another note telling them to put their dirty clothes and towels in the bag. I signed it the same way. That night, I found the red duffle bag, filled with laundry, neatly placed next to the washing machine! I was exuberant! I began to leave them lots of notes—not always with instructions—sometimes with donuts or hockey tickets. I let them know my expectations this way. But I also let them know, because of the title I gave myself, that I knew they were having difficulty accepting me, and that it was okay. I tried to keep it light, even to make it little bit fun."

Like Molly, many stepmothers who expect to be liked and accepted by their stepchildren feel that the burden of "likability" is theirs. When their stepchildren resist them, they try to appeal to them through treats, cute surprises and clever notes. They feel that even discipline has to be couched in terms of "fun." Although, like Molly, most eventually achieve *some* cooperation from their stepchildren, that cooperation remains optional, inconsistent and in the children's control. Ultimately, despite the occasional help they get with the laundry, their efforts prove less than satisfying.

Molly sums it up. "I guess I still hang onto the expectation that, someday, we'll feel like a family, instead of like a family and a stepmother. But, I confess that I'm beginning to see my stepsons as selfish. They consider only what *they* want. But the kids and I are stuck with each other, so we might as well make the best of it. And, who knows, they may come around someday. Maybe at my funeral they'll have something nice to say. Or maybe they'll just write my epitaph: Molly Jerome, dirty-rotten-no-good-but-loving-stepmother."

Rose Gardens, No Thorns

While the women discussed so far expected to like, love, rescue, hate or nurture their stepchildren, others' expectations focused on their stepchildren's feelings about *them*. Most, accustomed to successful relationships, expected that, with time and hard work, they would be "liked" and "accepted" by their stepchildren.

Many expected this acceptance to take time; their stepchildren would first have to adjust to their parents' breakups and their fathers' remarriages. Mia Jordan hoped that she could help her stepchildren deal with these changes. Nick and Amy were eight and four years old when she married their father, six years ago. "I assumed that the children would be somewhat less than thrilled to have me, rather than their mom, as their dad's wife. I expected that they'd resist getting to know me, and that their visits would be stressful for me *and* my husband, Bob, because they'd need him a lot. I also expected they'd be struggling with their emotions and that I'd have to help them adjust. And I thought their difficulties would evoke remorse from Bob, perhaps even homesickness for the family he'd left behind. I was sure that eventually I'd love them and they'd love me, given time and shared experiences and careful, honest communication."

Even when they expect stress and resistance, stepmothers like Mia often find themselves unprepared for the frustration they experience when they fail to gain acceptance by their stepchildren. They don't know how to behave when their stepchildren reject them. Mia was dumbfounded. "Normally, when someone meets a new person, there's a kid of unspoken, polite agreement that they'll each behave as if they want to get to know the other. Granted, Nick was only eight and Amy was just four, but they both completely ignored this convention and gave me no help in getting acquainted. I'd ask questions about school, movies, camp, books. Anything I could think of to find common ground. I'd get 'yup' and 'nope' answers, and neither of them would look me in the eye. They volunteered no information about their interests or opinions, and exhibited no curiosity about mine."

Stepmothers like Molly and Mia assume it is *their* responsibility to make their stepchildren like them and to make the relationships succeed. They try to convince their stepchildren that they are "okay" by filling their visits with entertainment, surprises and fun. Most of them, like Mia, find little or no success.

"We'd go to museums, circuses, movies and amusement parks," Mia recalls. "Nick and Amy are vegetarians, so I learned to cook vegetarian. Thirty ways to make eggplant. Tofu recipes galore. I know more things to do with beans than you'd ever imagine. I shopped, cooked, cleaned and entertained, and at the end of the weekend, they'd say, 'Thanks, Dad,' and kiss Bob goodbye. I never got a 'thank you' unless Bob took them aside and *told* them to thank me. In six years, I never got a kiss back if I gave one. I never received a voluntary hug. Christmas and birthdays found *me* shopping for *their* gifts. But I never got even a *card* from them—they'd put 'and Mia' on the envelope with their Dad's gift. Like I could use a tie tack."

Many women in situations like Mia's feel that their stepchildren address them only when they want something. They hesitate to complain about running errands and doing chores for their step-children, given the deep emotional upheaval the children have been through. Nevertheless, they feel used. "The only time they speak to me is when they ask me to do something," one complains. "The routine is, 'I forgot my bathing suit, can you buy me one?' 'I forgot my pajamas, toothpaste, hairbrush, shampoo, gloves, socks, book . . . can you buy me one?' It sounds petty to dwell on toothbrushes and barrettes when you consider the sadness they're dealing with. But it's like a mosquito bite, constantly annoying. Whenever they visit, I *know* I'll end up shopping for things their mother hasn't bothered to pack."

Eventually, many of these stepmothers find that their determination to "love and be loved" by their stepchildren wears out. Instead of fondness or even appreciation, they feel that their stepchildren show increasing contempt for them. They describe themselves as being treated like "hired help" or "intruders" in their own homes. Over time, some, like Mia, give up.

"Finally, after a few years of trying and getting nowhere, I backed off. I stopped cooking. I ordered pizza. What I'd *expected* might be difficult about being a stepmother was helping the children deal with profound emotional conflicts. I'd been prepared for tears and fears and insecurities. What I got was chilly silence, extra chores and a bunch of bills."

Stepmothers who try to win the affections of their stepchildren *often* find that their efforts are unsuccessful and unappreciated. Their expectations of being liked and accepted as part of the family are seldom realized. In fact, the harder they try, the more pressure they feel to "succeed," and the more difficult their relationships with their stepchildren often become. Frustrated, many begin to resent their efforts to please the children. Some, like Mia, retreat; others, like Molly, lower their expectations of their relationships. Either way, it is, at least in part, their own initially high expectations of warm relationships with their stepchildren that, ironically, set them up for rejection or failure.

Love, Honor and Obedience

So far, the expectations described by stepmothers have concerned their relationships with their stepchildren. A number of others, however, consider their stepmother roles to be primarily subcategories or offshoots of their marital responsibilities. Their expectations often reveal fears and insecurities that they hide from their spouses. Some expect difficulties because of the power their stepchildren have over their husbands; others worry about the effects of their husbands' deep-seated guilts. Most say that their expectations prove accurate, but that reality is even more drastic than they had anticipated. In fact, their husbands often *demand* that they "perform well" as stepmothers, that they "please" their stepchildren, even that they behave, in some cases, as subordinate extensions of paternal authority rather than as individuals in and of themselves.

Among those women who expected that being a "good stepmother" would be a requirement of their marriages are several who confide that their husbands have no idea how they really feel about being stepmothers. They are unsure that their marriages can withstand the truth about those feelings. Because they believe that conflicts with their stepchildren have the potential to destroy their marriages, they put up fronts of happiness and harmony to mask their true emotions. These women call themselves "chickens," "martyrs" and "hypocrites," but see honesty as too great a risk.

Jennifer Slade, forty, is a public relations specialist. She hesitates to talk about being a stepmother because she doesn't want her husband or her fifteen-year-old stepson to recognize her story. "My husband couldn't accept me if he knew how I actually feel about his son," she explains. "You see, my expectations had more to do with being a good *wife* than a good *stepmother*. But, clearly, the two went hand in hand. My husband's happiness was tied to his son, David. So, from the start, I did whatever I could to make David happy. I treated him like a bed-and-board guest. He didn't have to pick up a sock, let alone make his bed. I committed myself to making David feel like royalty in our home to please my husband."

Most women who deliberately extend themselves to their step-children expect nothing in return. Often, *nothing* is exactly what they receive. This response may be due to the fact that their stepchildren, fully aware of their power, take advantage of their stepmothers' determination to please them. Another contributing factor, however, may be that these stepmothers see their stepchildren merely as vehicles through which they can please their husbands, rather than as individuals with whom they want to build independent relationships. Under these circumstances, it is hardly surprising that their relationships are strained and their roles within the stepfamilies seem false.

"We play a lot," Jennifer reports. "We play at being a family, but we aren't. I play the cheerful innkeeper, but I'm not. All I've ever really wanted is my husband and my privacy. Instead, I got David. Lots of David."

Many women like Jennifer feel trapped by their roles and powerless to assert themselves. They complain that their homes are always open to their stepchildren, that there is no privacy or time reserved exclusively for their marriages. They are afraid even to *try* to set limits of any kind because they don't think their husbands would support them.

Jennifer remembers taking an afternoon off work last summer. "I'd planned that afternoon for a month. I was going to read a novel and laze around like a potted plant.

"While I was on the porch, reading, David rode up on his bike. He plopped onto the hammock and asked for a glass of juice. I was

outraged at the intrusion, but afraid to ask him, however gently, to
leave, or even to get his own juice. I didn't, and don't, want to upset
him and risk a confrontation with my husband. So, I seethed in silence
and served David lemonade and cookies. He stuck around for most of
the afternoon. I felt like a caged animal."

Many women assume that if they alienate their stepchildren, they
will alienate their husbands. This assumption forces them to accept a
subordinate role in the family, play servant to their stepchildren and
feign happiness for the sake of their marriages. Because they are afraid
of their stepchildren's power, they placate them, perpetuating the very
situations that plague them. Because they define "good stepmother"
in terms of how well they please their stepchildren and husbands, they
end up infuriating *themselves*. And, because they deliberately hide
their feelings from their husbands, they actively contribute to their
own problems.

Teamwork

Jennifer is by no means unique in her decision to conceal her
feelings about her stepson from her husband. Almost half of the
women we interviewed said that, although they are happily married,
they don't expect their husbands to fully understand their feelings
about stepmothering. Many say they've tried to protect their husbands
from conflicts involving their stepchildren. But some describe situations in which such conflicts are encouraged, if not created, by the
husbands themselves.

Initially, most of these stepmothers expected to be treated as equals
in their marriages and in their parenting teams. In reality, however,
they feel ignored or even invisible when their stepchildren are around.
Whether consciously or not their husbands and stepchildren habitually
exclude them from activities and conversations. If this exclusion is ever
mentioned, their husbands defensively deny it; some even blame their
wives for jealously trying to interfere in their already unstable
relationships with their children.

Jamie Simpkins became tired of the power plays conducted by her
stepdaughter, Brittany. "One day, it dawned on me why my husband
became a marshmallow every time Brittany came over: he was

terrified of angering her, of losing her to her mother. He gave in to her all the time, so that what *I* wanted didn't matter. All that mattered was what Brittany wanted. When I realized that Keith was basing his decision about having another child on Brittany's reaction to the idea, I knew my marriage was at stake. I took action. Brittany could no longer rule my life."

Jamie, like others, finally decided to take matters into her own hands, dealing directly with her stepchild, instead of with or through her husband.

"It was simple, actually," Jamie remembers. "I decided to treat Brittany just as she'd been treating me. When she came over to visit one weekend, I knew Keith would be gone all afternoon. I invited a friend over, and my friend and I simply ignored her, just the way she and her father regularly ignored me. I baked a pie, but didn't include her. I laughed and joked with my friend, but when Brittany made a comment, we paid no attention. Finally she broke. In tears, she screamed that she hated me. Pushing her to the breaking point wasn't the beginning I'd *wanted*, but that outburst started my relationship with Brittany.

"We spent the next several hours talking. I told her how left out I felt from her life, and that being left out upset me the same way it upset her. We talked for a long time. She sobbed about her parents. I don't remember everything I said, but it must have been okay because the tension dissipated and we began, after years of battling each other, to be friends."

When women like Jamie realize that their husbands are the source of the conflicts between them and their stepchildren, some dare to eliminate tensions by directly, sometimes dramatically, confronting their stepchildren. In doing so, they not only establish their own power base in the family, but also open direct communications with their stepchildren, clear the air and lay the foundations for subsequent relationships. Many who take these risks find that their stepchildren are relieved to have limits and open communication, and that they accept their stepmothers' authority willingly.

"My expectation today," Jamie remarks, "is not about Keith, our parenting team *or* about my status as his partner. Today, it's about Brittany, that she and I will remain friends. Our relationship began only because we both loved Keith. But, slowly the relationship began to include *us*, even to be based on us. Now that I'm not so angry, I can see the pain, loneliness and fear of abandonment she'd been suffering. I don't know that I'll ever be able to rid her of those feelings, but now, at least, I can listen and let her know I care."

Happily Ever After

Some stepmothers start out simply expecting "happy families" in which they will love and nurture their stepchildren. Although their husbands often share these expectations and work with them to try to create "happy families," their stepchildren resist. Most couples persevere, fighting this resistance and trying to lure the children into positive relationships. But some find that the children can't bear even to *see* their fathers' new homes, let alone to participate in activities there.

Jill Sterling's stepson, Charlie, was seven years old when she married his father, Michael. "Charlie refused to enter our house. He was sullen and silent and, for the first few years of our marriage, he literally would not cross our threshold. Charlie finally told us why, but it took lots of prodding.

"Charlie couldn't bear to see the rugs, sofa and dining-room set that had been in his parents' house in ours. Our furniture looked to him like a neon sign flashing, 'DIVORCE!'"

Stepmothers like Jill, sensitive to their stepchildren's feelings, devote themselves to helping the children work their problems out. Most are so focused on their stepchildren that they do not even mention their own feelings or reactions to their stepchildren's resistance. In order to help their stepchildren solve their problems, they willingly restructure their priorities and rearrange their lives.

Jill, for example, eased Charlie through his difficult adjustment period by spending their visits entirely *outside* the home, at the zoo, museums or movies. "Eventually, after about two years, Charlie finally agreed to enter our house. He came in, but wouldn't go beyond the foyer. This went on for months. We didn't know what to do. We brought him his meals there and ate picnic-style with him on the floor. His attitude didn't change. So, we tried *not* catering to him. We stopped bringing him his meals. That didn't work, either. Charlie skipped lunch rather than enter our house. Gradually, Michael and I got discouraged."

Like Jill, many stepmothers begin to feel defeated when their heartfelt efforts to befriend their stepchildren meet with continued resistance. Some find that the resulting frustration takes a toll on their marriages, depressing and sapping the energy of both partners. Others, however, grow closer to their husbands and affirm their commitments through their joint efforts at dealing with the stepchildren's problems. Jill and Michael, for example, spent hours planning strategies to coax Charlie into their living room. In the process, they became a team, holding endless discussions and reading books on child psychology, divorce and stepfamilies. However, even the most devoted stepmothers with the best intentions and supportive husbands sometimes discover that there *are* limits. If their efforts to build "happy families" fail, some eventually give up and let their stepchildren define their relationships. Others, after years of investing time and emotion that lead nowhere, find themselves increasingly vulnerable to their stepchildren's rejection. And a few, like Jill, find that a seemingly minor incident can change their attitudes completely.

"We'd taken Charlie and his cousin, Pete, on a vacation to Florida. We were outside, at a show with dolphins and whales. It was windy and my husband's hair was mussed. I reached over to smooth it back in place with an affectionate gesture.

"Out of the corner of my eye, I saw Charlie imitate me. Not just imitate—mock. He swooned and batted his eyelashes. I was mortified. I became instantly self-conscious, as if I had to be careful not to give him material to mimic. I'd *never* thought of Charlie as anything but a *victim* before. But, after that day, I felt like he was also a bratty little judge."

Stepmothers whose feelings change with a single incident usually realize that the incident itself is not the *real* cause of the change. Most, quite simply, are burned out, exhausted and sometimes quite angry. Many sadly conclude that their expectations of happy, loving families are "absurd," "unattainable," or "a dream." They say that, by putting their stepchildren's needs above their own, they and their husbands have created imbalances in the structures of their families. They see themselves as "the dumping ground" for their stepchildren's angers and feel "rejected," "personally invisible" or "used."

Most who simply expect to be part of "happy families" soon describe their expectations as naive. Like Jill, many learn that their stepchildren's picture of a happy family includes the children, their father and mother, but *not* their stepmother. Often, it is only when they accept this difference in family ideals and admit to their *own* unhappiness that they take their first steps toward achieving more realistic, mature and attainable sets of stepmothering goals.

Tug-of-War

Even when stepchildren do accept their stepmothers as part of the family, the relationships formed are usually far too complex to be labeled "happy." Fully half of the stepmothers who simply expected loving, happy families say that they have become caught in never-ending, energy-draining battles of wills with their stepchildren. In waging these battles, stepchildren often employ impressive weapons, including self-destructive behaviors. As stepchildren get older, many outgrow their desires to fight with their stepmothers. Just as often, however, the older the stepchildren are, the more precise, subtle and powerful their weapons become.

Some stepmothers are caught in battles with their formidable adult stepchildren. They say that their husbands are no help, since they, too, are usually victims of the struggle. A few of these women finally get so angered that they declare martial law, risking their relationships with their stepchildren and, in some cases, their marriages, in order to maintain an uneasy peace on their own turfs.

Marla Jenson has two adult stepchildren, Tiffany and Eric, now twenty-six and twenty-two, who have fought to control the family ever since she married their father eight years ago. "I expected the Brady Bunch," Marla jokes. "What I got was a stepson who is determined to fail at everything, just so he can prove that his father and I have ruined his life, and a stepdaughter who milks her father for every cent she can, as if someday he *might* write the check that finally buys her love."

Many stepmothers expect that their adult stepchildren will be independent and not heavily involved with their fathers' new families. Often, however, this is not the case. Even adult stepchildren can be financially or emotionally dependent on their fathers, taking advantage of their fathers' hospitality, vulnerability or generosity.

Stepmothers like Marla find their adult stepchildren refusing to accept adult responsibilities. Instead of taking on challenges and progressing with their lives, they appear to be stuck, focusing on past events, and looking for excuses for not growing up. Their specific problems vary, but they tend to blame their fathers for *whatever* troubles they have, and they often expect "Dad" to "make up" for any and all emotional or developmental "damage" they experienced in their childhoods.

As "Dad's wife," these women are caught between their husbands' loving guilts and their stepchildren's punishing manipulations. If they assert themselves by standing up to their stepchildren, chances are that their husbands will side with the children.

"My stepson, Eric, alternates between getting thrown out and dropping out of the expensive schools we send him to. He lies and uses drugs. He can't hold a job. My husband, Steve, worries himself sick, but Eric *blames* Steve, claiming his life was ruined by his parents' divorce, which he sees as all his father's fault. Eric insists that he lost all his self-esteem and motivation when Steve left. So, it follows that it's his *father's* fault that Eric doesn't study or work. It's his *father's* fault that he takes drugs. Everything he does to destroy his life is his father's fault. Nobody can persuade him otherwise.

"My stepdaughter, Tiffany, is even more difficult, though. Last summer she was taking a graduate course about ten minutes from our house. We pay Tiffany's rent in an expensive, high-rise apartment in town. But from *there*, her class would have been a twenty-minute commute—*in the car her father bought for her*—and she thought that was too far. So, she decided to camp out in our living room for the whole summer, just to save ten minutes commuting time. Her father welcomed her, because he wanted his family together. But when I came home from work, hot and exhausted, I'd find Tiffany lounging in her underwear on the sofabed, her shoes and clothes scattered everywhere, and she'd glance up from a magazine or phone conversation to ask what was for dinner. I remember telling her, one day, to cook or order herself a pizza, that I wasn't Donna Reed. She glared at me and answered back that I'd 'have to' cook for her father, anyway. I nearly lost it."

Stepmothers who find themselves pushed around by their adult stepchildren sometimes decide to take some positive action in order to end the battle of wills. Some withdraw from the contest, refusing to participate in stepfamily activities, except on their own terms. Others, like Marla, find that a showdown is needed.

"The final straw came when a friend of mine from out of town wanted to visit. Tiffany refused to vacate the sofabed, even for one night. That was it. I'd had it. I insisted that she get out. I shouted, 'This is my *home* not a dormitory'" She screamed back at me and ran around throwing her things into suitcases, and I ran after her, helping her empty drawers, tossing clothes at her. It was *awful!* But I got my living room back. And I let Tiffany know, with no doubts in her mind, that *I* was in charge, at least in my own home. Steve was furious. Tiffany was hysterical. But I slept better that night than I had all summer."

Women who decide to assert themselves in the family often find their husbands furious with them for upsetting their stepchildren. Some risk their marriages in order to win decisive battles with their stepchildren. Many, though, believe that, unless they wage these battles, their marriages will eventually be at risk anyway.

Most are convinced that their showdowns permanently change their status in the family. Their adult stepchildren learn that, although their fathers might endlessly pamper them, their stepmothers will *not.* The short-term outcomes of these showdowns often include tense relations and strained communications. However, as wounded feelings heal, relationships and communication pick up on a new basis in which the children are afraid to push their stepmothers too far. These assertive stepmothers see themselves, in some ways, as their husbands' protectors. They believe, too, that the limits they set, even through unpleasant confrontations, are actually for the stepchildren's benefit, since they require them to act like adults and to accept responsibility for their own lives. Further, many find that these explosions *can* be cathartic, breaking destructive patterns and leading to more positive ones once family members have vented pent-up resentments and been forced to acknowledge each other's feelings.

"I still don't have the Brady Bunch," Marla admits. "But I don't have aggravation, either. And I don't *expect* the Brady Bunch anymore. I don't even expect to be appreciated, let alone liked. Instead, I expect to look after myself and *my* needs; to protect *my* home and my *own* interests. I realize that the hold my stepchildren have on my husband is very deep; I can't fight that. But, by staking out my turf and taking control of the part of his life that is me and our daughter, I've stopped being a punching bag. I'm even developing peace of mind."

Friends

Although some stepmothers expected to be friends with their stepchildren, they actually hoped to be more. Among these are women who had hoped for so much that they knew they were risking disappointment. Typically, they had held two sets of expectations: "ideal" and "real." They hoped to accomplish their idealistic ones and were determined to achieve their realistic ones. Often, they failed at both.

Maxine James married Gordon four years ago when her stepdaughter was just seven. "Ideally, I hoped I'd save Tina from the damage she'd suffered from having an incompetent, neglectful mother. I hoped I could become a positive role model for Tina, even though I didn't see myself as *replacing* her mother in any way.

"On the more realistic end, I expected 'girl stuff,' you know, shopping and talking and polishing nails and styling hair. I didn't expect her to *love* me, but I expected she'd return some kind of warmth.

Maxine pauses. "Somewhere along the line, we messed up. It's failed at both counts."

Stepmothers who seek to attain ideal relationships with their stepchildren, usually find it impossible to do so, due to forces beyond their control. Some find that their stepchildren's mothers provide obstacles to their relationships. Others discover that their husbands' ideals for their relationships differ from, or are even mutually exclusive with, their own. A few find that their blossoming steprelationships are disrupted or destroyed when they have their *own* children. Most find that more than one complicating factor obstructs their efforts, but that the greatest blockages to their ideal relationships are provided by the stepchildren themselves.

"My relationship with my stepdaughter is measured by how much I can do for her," Maxine says. "If Tina wants something, she's a peach. Otherwise, she's ice."

Stepmothers like Maxine find that their husbands complicate

matters by trying to force their relationship with their stepchildren. "Gordon never seems to think I do enough for Tina. He wants us to include her in everything we do, and pressures me to think of her as my own daughter. I *can't* think of her that way, but I do my best to please Gordon, even though it means I've turned into Tina's slave. I'm always trying to prove how much I care about her, or that I treat her the same way I treat my daughter, Ruthie. I feel defensive, like I have to *prove* that I'm a good stepmother. No matter what I do, I seem to fall short."

When stepmothers' initial goals continually elude their grasps, criticism from their husbands exacerbates their own sense of failure. The longer and harder their stepchildren's resistance, the more pressure they feel to overcome it, and the more frustrated they feel if they cannot.

"Obviously," Maxine concedes, "the cozy relationship I expected isn't to be. I'm not Tina's role model and I can't even get her to do 'girl stuff' with me. Still, every so often, I gather up my energy and tell Tina I love her. She brushes me off with appropriate words. I extend myself only for her to reject me. And Gordon insists that I consider her my own. I can't feel what Gordon wants me to feel; I can't be whatever Tina needs me to be; I can't get what I want in terms of our family. It wears me out."

Eventually, many women like Maxine find themselves exhausted by their continued failures to establish bonds with their stepchildren. Some are afraid of disappointing their husbands. Others worry about abandoning their stepchildren to the influence of destructive or incompetent mothers. Most, however, feel that by offering friendship to their stepchildren, they are repeatedly inviting rejection. Accordingly, their expectations of friendship or of "sugar and spice things" dissolve, replaced by expectations of disappointment and a continuing sense of failure.

Expectations

Only a fifth of the women we interviewed find that the reality of their experiences as stepmothers is better than their expectations. Those who are disappointed, universally say that their presence in the family is resented and resisted by their stepchildren and that their husbands, for a variety of reasons, lack the inclination or the power to improve the situation.

Overall, the specific nature of the disappointment stepmothers experience falls into four main, sometimes overlapping areas. First, like Maggie, Maxine and Julie, there are those who are surprised at how little appreciation or satisfaction they receive from their step-children for their efforts.

Next, like Marla, Jennifer and Molly, some complain that they feel "used" or "invaded" by stepchildren who are basically "lazy," "self-centered" and "greedy."

Third, stepmothers like Maxine, Jamie and Jennifer are disap-pointed in their husbands' inability or unwillingness to work with them or even to be supportive of them.

Finally, like Mia and Jill, some women are "ignored" or "not recognized as individuals" to the point that they feel resentful and "invisible."

In every area, however, there are some women who are able to achieve a degree of satisfaction or peace by letting go of their original expectations and accepting reality.

Once they accept the reality of their situations, some stepmothers are able to make their roles more tolerable, or even pleasant, by taking charge and establishing some parameters. Some, like Mia, Jessie and Jill, accomplish this by backing out rather than trying to force relationships with their stepchildren. Some, like Jamie and Marla, precipitate confrontations that jolt family members into dealing with each other openly. And some, like Molly, Julie and Marla, assert their authority by setting limits.

Those who are able to set limits manage not only to establish a degree of status in the family, but also to gain a sense of strength with regard to their stepchildren, their husbands and their own lives.

The stepmothers who remain the most troubled by their roles are those who have not, for a variety of reasons, been able to abandon their initial expectations. Like Maxine and Jennifer, they struggle in vain to make reality conform to expectation, regardless of the expense, in energy and emotion, to themselves.

Advice From Stepmothers on Expectations

1.   **Try not to have any.** Whatever you expect, things will probably be different. Be flexible and ready for anything. Observe and

listen before you form expectations, much less commitments. Expect the unexpected.

2.   **Be patient.** Don't expect to realize your expectations, if you have any, right away. Allow time for adjustments and readjustments. It will take time for your stepchildren to become accustomed to you and for your relationships to grow.

3.   **Communicate.** Talk with your stepchildren and your husband about your mutual expectations as early as possible in your relationships. Then, keep the conversations going, as expectations are met, disappointed or changed.

THREE

A Day in the Life

When we began our interviews, we assumed that physical custody would be the main factor determining the degree to which a step-mother's daily life was influenced by her stepchildren. We expected that women whose stepchildren lived with them would be more heavily affected than those whose stepchildren lived with their mothers.

We learned, however, that this is not necessarily the case. Step-mothers whose stepchildren live with them usually do more laundry and cook more meals than others, but, eventually, they also fall into routines which, while dominated by the stepchildren, allow them to adjust to their presence.

Stepmothers whose stepchildren come and go, on the other hand, often find that their daily lives are profoundly changed or disrupted by the children's visits. The most intrusive effects of the visits are usually emotional, rather than physical. "It's not about washing dishes," said one. "It's about dealing with everybody's underlying, often compet-ing, needs and getting used to being with each other all over again, each time they come."

Stepmothering affects most women's daily lives primarily in terms of personal territory, children's activities and authority. *Personal territory* includes personal space, time, privacy and possessions. *Children's activities* refers to the amount stepmothers participate in their stepchildren's affairs. *Authority* means the degree to which stepmothers feel it is not only their responsibility but also their prerogative to initiate various aspects of parenting, including discipline.

Most stepmothers find their stepchildren have such an immense impact on their daily lives that it's difficult to define or separate the issues. Nevertheless, the vast majority of stepmothers have problems with authority. These problems arise for some because their step-children resist or resent their authority; for others, because their husbands deny them the ability to reward, discipline or assert any kind of parental control. But most stepmothers who have difficulty with authority attribute the source of the problem to *themselves*. They struggle internally about how much authority they *should* accept for their husbands' children, or how much they, personally, can handle.

Personal territory is an especially touchy subject for stepmothers whose stepchildren live with them. For many, personal territory simply does not exist; every moment of their day is subject to interruption or invasion. Similarly, over half of the stepmothers whose stepchildren regularly visit stated they have no control over their daily routines when the children are there; personal space and privacy disappear and the children's activities take priority. These women complain of a seesaw element in their daily lives, with the emphasis shifting back and forth from personal goals and marriage to step-children and their activities. They describe never-ending efforts to find a balance between their own day-to-day priorities and those of their stepchildren.

Open Arms

A number of the women we interviewed stated that they do not mind interruptions or intrusions by their stepchildren at all; in fact, they welcome them. Many of these women have no children of their own and find that the role of stepmother gives them the opportunity to experience nurturing and maternal roles. But even some of those *with* children feel this way. They experience more freedom in the role of stepmother than in that of mother; as stepmothers, they can relax and enjoy their relationships without the worry and responsibility of parenthood.

Women in this group create various types of relationships. Some choose to be "pals" with their stepchildren; a few try to be "fairy godmothers"; others maintain more structured relationships, such as "advisors" or part-time "caretakers." What these women share, however, is that they themselves define their roles. The relationships they offer their stepchildren are based upon these self-determined roles; the only choice left to their stepchildren is that of accepting or rejecting the relationship. Because these stepmothers offer relationships that are comfortable for *them*, they don't experience their stepchildren's presence as invasive or intrusive. And, if the stepchildren refuse the relationships, they do not alter their offers.

Molly Jerome is most comfortable with an active, generous, somewhat mischievous role. She never hesitates to invade her stepsons' lives with the unexpected. She leaves surprise packages in their rooms when they visit and goes out of her way to make them have fun. One of her recent projects consisted of decorating her house in a Spanish motif, cooking Spanish food and talking Spanish from a phrase book during meals because one of her stepsons was nervous about his Spanish final.

Molly explains her attitude this way, "Look, I'm certainly not their peer, but I'm not their parent either. And I don't want to compete with their parents. I tease my stepchildren. I tell them they're lucky to have me in their lives, because I don't have to be in charge of discipline and rules or serious stuff with them. I tell them it's up to *them* to decide what our relationship should be. We can be friends, or not. We can have fun, or not. We can trust each other, or not. We have the opportunity to *choose*. I tell them they can choose as much or as little from me as they want. But I don't really leave it up to them. I keep reminding them of my affection. I send goodie boxes to them at camp, or cupcakes to their class at school. I reaffirm my fondness for them every chance I get. My consistent message is that I care about them, but it's *their* choice what they want from me."

Women like Molly often devote lots of time and effort to their stepchildren, but ask or expect little in return. Those without their own children are happy just to have children in their lives and are prepared to wait years, if necessary, for their stepchildren to return their affection. But, despite their consistency, patience and persistent efforts, most encounter resistance, even hostility, from their stepchildren, at least initially.

Molly recalls that her stepsons once found football jerseys she'd bought them as a surprise and accused her of trying to "buy" them. Like many others who have encountered similarly suspicious attitudes, Molly felt hurt and frustrated, but she did not give up. "I told them what I always tell them: 'If you decide to take the time to get to know me, you'll find out that it's just my nature to give. It gives me pleasure to put a smile on your face.' But I learned that I can't push too hard or I crowd them. The boys need to take their time and make their own decisions."

Some of these stepmothers find that their patience and consistency eventually pays off. One spent weeks painting by numbers with her stepsons. "I wanted their visits to be fun for them. They liked painting, so I painted. I did what they did. I have a basement full of awful artwork now, but those sticky oil paintings helped glue us together and I treasure each one of them!"

Although these stepmothers work hard at their relationships, they feel no *external* pressure to do so. Whatever pressure they feel is self-inflicted. Their husbands appreciate and encourage their efforts, but neither push nor demand. Like Molly, many work to create fun or entertainment *not* because they feel fun is required or expected of them, but because they believe that light-hearted experiences will bring them closer to their stepchildren.

Unlike many others, these stepmothers experience a clear sense of their own power. They *choose* their roles and degrees of involvement. They *enjoy* being stepmothers. While few of them say they have as yet achieved the secure, solid relationships they seek with their stepchildren, most believe these relationship will develop, eventually. Like Molly, they hope that their affection and consistency will be rewarded someday, and, meanwhile, they accept the process of waiting.

At Arm's Length

Not all stepmothers welcome their stepchildren into their personal territory. Just as some allow their stepchildren all the space they want, others feel that *any* space occupied by their stepchildren is too much. Haunted by the idea that their husbands are forever bound to the past through their offspring, a small percentage of women completely reject their stepchildren, fully aware of the destructive effects this may have on their stepfamilies, their marriages or even their own well-being. Some rationalize their jealous behavior as a sign of "romantic values" instead of "emotional problems." Certainly, these women are extremely unhappy to be stepmothers.

Jessie Solomon, whose stepchildren are grown, avoids family gatherings and other events that involve her stepchildren. She doesn't visit them or allow her husband, Mark, to invite them to their home. The very *idea* of her stepchildren upsets her so deeply that she gets stomachaches when she knows she has to see them and begins trembling when people ask about or discuss them in public. Despite the fact that she has all but banished them from her daily life, Jessie says her stepchildren still invade her personal territory in a major way.

"Whether I see them or not," Jessie explains, "I feel their presence whenever my husband's attention focuses on them. I feel invaded when they call on the phone. I feel an undercurrent, a constant threat. Are they going to come between us today? Is Mark going to speak to them? Is Mark thinking about them? The degree to which I'm affected by them is unnerving, but it's because I know how deeply Mark loves them."

By eliminating their stepchildren from their personal territory, women like Jessie affect their entire families' interactions. They rob their stepchildren of contact with their fathers and *themselves* of potentially happy families. The stress of these situations upsets both their stomachs and the foundations of their daily lives. These women exhaust themselves fighting realities they cannot change: their stepchildren, whether they like it or not, exist. Although they realize that refusing to deal with this existence and their own problems is not a solution, these stepmothers seem unable to do anything else.

Unarmed

The great majority of stepmothers fall between the two extremes: those who welcome stepchildren with open arms and those who banish them completely. In general, those who have the authority to set limits and to define their relationships feel happier about having stepchildren than those who don't. And those who *don't* often blame their lack of authority on their husbands.

Most who blame their husbands saw warning signs early in their marriages, but thought things would change. They made excuses, assuming that their husbands were trying to help their stepchildren adjust to having a new adult in the family. Jennifer Slade remembers patiently allowing her husband to put her stepson's wishes first in every situation, expecting that it would be only a matter of time before she would become part of the parenting team.

"I remember sitting in a Chinese restaurant, gritting my teeth while Alex let my stepson, David, order our entire meal. It hit me that night that I was jealous of David, and not because he'd decided what I would eat for dinner. I was jealous of David's status in the family and in my husband's life. I wanted my husband to focus his attention on me as intensely as he did on David."

Stepmothers like Jennifer often enter their marriages without understanding how their husbands see the role of stepmother. "When I married Alex," Jennifer recalls, "he said he wanted me to be David's stepmother, to participate in his upbringing and to be emotionally involved with him. That sounded wonderful.

"What Alex *meant*, though, was not that he wanted me as an equal partner, sharing parental responsibilities, but that he wanted an assistant, a second-string person, a backup. He wanted me to enhance *his* relationship with his son, not to create my own."

Stepmothers in situations like Jennifer's often feel that their husbands unconsciously encourage a rivalry between them and their stepchildren. Unsure of where they rank in the competition, most are reluctant to challenge their stepchildren in any way that might precipitate confrontations, especially by setting limits or enforcing discipline. They feel that they cannot discuss these issues because their husbands see their attempts to establish independent authority as betrayal. In order to placate their husbands, therefore, these women try to keep their stepchildren happy by keeping their own needs and opinions to themselves. They describe themselves as powerless, even as "enslaved."

"Ironically, *because* I craved my husband's attention so much, I tried desperately to please him," Jennifer explains. "And, since pleasing him meant pleasing his son, I pleased his son.

"This pattern continues, even today. At my worst moments, I think David's not only aware of his power but smug about it. Sometimes, when our eyes meet, I see a look in David's eyes that challenges me— like, 'Don't get in my way, Jennifer, or you'll regret it.' I'm not *sure* he intends that message. Maybe I infer it because I'm so upset. Actually, it's Alex who's the problem. It's Alex, not David, who's supposed to set limits for his son and be a husband and partner to me."

Because stepmothers like Jennifer have no authority to set limits, their personal territory is completely open to their stepchildren. Their husbands insist that they meet their stepchildren's needs or whims, and most silently comply because they don't want to cause trouble. One stepmother says that mayhem broke out when she told her husband she didn't want her stepchildren to go out with them for her birthday. "I wanted to be alone with my husband. But he became so furious when I suggested that we get a sitter for his kids that I asked him what he wanted from me. I'll never forget his reply. Coldly, he told me the simple, unbearable truth about his vision of me as a stepmother: 'I want you to participate and do as you're told!'"

Women in similar circumstances believe that their marriages will be threatened if they confront their husbands about their stepchildren. At first, many waited, hoping they could talk things out calmly as a couple and eventually define the scope of their stepfamily relationships together. However, they found that such an opportunity never arose.

Most of these women do not see their husbands as ogres; in fact, most of them claim to be happily married. The conflicts they experience arise only where their stepchildren are concerned, and only if they contradict their husbands by wanting, for example, increased privacy or authority. For many, marriage would be perfect if their husbands didn't change when their stepchildren appeared. "Whenever David's around," Jennifer complains, "Alex becomes a stranger. He acts almost as if he's embarrassed by me. We can be snuggled on the sofa, reading, sipping wine, listening to music, when David drops over. Five minutes later, some hockey or football game is blaring on TV, David and Alex are shouting cheers, and I'm in the kitchen making popcorn."

An upsetting side effect experienced by some of these stepmothers is that their self-images become damaged by their lack of status in the family. Although many consciously decide to allow their husbands and stepchildren to dominate, their passive roles slowly and insidiously eat away at their self-esteem.

One stepmother says, "In my own life, I don't rank first or even second—I barely make it to third. I come in someplace after my stepchild and after my husband's career. Andrea is the omnipresent, omnipotent stepchild. She's the focus of our lives. Usually, I feel like my feelings don't matter."

Although they claim that they *choose* passivity over the upheaval that assertiveness might cause, those stepmothers who strive to maintain the peace in the family by stifling their own needs often find that peace costs them dearly. Many say that they know they "should work on their marriages" or that they plan to participate in marital therapy "someday." But awareness of their options, or even of the part they themselves play in their own unhappiness, does not necessarily lead them to alter their behavior. Some rationalize their situations, suggesting that "many problems have no clear solutions," or that they must balance what they give to a relationship with what they get from it. Whatever their rationalizations, many stepmothers remain unwilling either to reveal their feelings to their husbands or to assert themselves with their stepchildren because they believe they'll risk all if they do. Unprepared to take that risk, they choose to struggle with frustration, anger and sometimes humiliation, simply because these are knowns that seem safe.

Arm in Arm

Some women whose husbands try to control their relationships with their stepchildren flatly refuse to allow it. Like Jennifer, they understand that their husbands are insecure about their postdivorce relationships with their children and that they try to prevent them from asserting authority or controlling personal territory because they are threatened by anyone who comes between them and their children, even their own wives. However, when their husbands jealously try to dominate or exclude them, some stepmothers do not react passively; rather, they actively, often ingeniously, build their stepmother roles and relationships *around*, rather than *with*, their husbands.

"If someone had asked me about my personal space during the first few years of my marriage, I'd probably have cried," Jamie Simpkins recalls. "I had no personal territory. Everything was invaded by my stepdaughter, Brittany. I was jealous of her exclusivity with my husband and I resented her and was miserable every time she visited. Now, after ten years, I still have no personal space, but it's because I've pulled Brittany in. Now, I *want* it this way. I often find Brittany in my closet, rifling through my stuff, trying to find some shirt or sweater I've borrowed and forgotten to return. Personal territory? Forget it! I know I'll never see my silver Indian earrings again, except on *her* ears. But then, she's not likely to get back that Guatemalan scarf, so it evens out."

Stepmothers like Jamie find it possible to create successful relationships with their stepchildren only when these relationships are formed outside their husbands' realms. The authority they hold is self-proclaimed; the nature and scope of their roles are self-determined. Although they are often frustrated and angry that they can't work *with* their husbands in forming their stepfamilies, these women are also unwilling to be shut out. Most important, they are motivated and confident enough to commit themselves to forming independent relationships with their stepchildren.

"Brittany and I have become friends, as much as a forty-year-old and a sixteen-year-old *can* be friends." Jamie smiles. "But it wasn't easy to get to this point. We spent lots of tears and took lots of risks, exposing our feelings and fears in intense confrontations. It took work, by *both* of us. So what we have is by no means superficial. We talk about her boyfriend, relationships, values, family, sex, religion, everything. We talk about her goals. She's asked me about law school and I think she's considering the law as a profession and it thrills me, because I know I'm the role model for that—I'm the only attorney in the family."

The happy relationships experienced by stepmothers like Jamie, however, are often not without strains. As wives, these women feel that they are "sneaking" around, trying to hide their relationships with their stepchildren from their husbands. Jamie says that her relationship with Brittany sometimes seems like a gentle conspiracy against her husband, Keith. "Brit and I giggle about private jokes and Keith doesn't know why. Or, she and I tease Keith—affectionately—about the same things. In his presence, Brittany will say something to me like, 'Do you see what Dad is *wearing* today?! What ever possessed him to put *that* shirt and *those* pants on at the same time?' Keith becomes, at these times, like our pet, or our beloved macho mascot. But we protect him, because we love him and we know he can't deal with us both at the same time."

Stepmothers like Jamie have made conscious compromises and

adjustments in order to keep their husbands happy and their step-children close. Rather than trying to change their husbands' attitudes in order to attain their own concept of "family," they accept their husbands' needs for exclusivity with their children. But these women do not allow their husbands' needs to isolate or disempower them. Instead, they work independently within their husbands' frameworks to build their own relationships and strengthen their families. In doing so, many of them feel that the rewards are mixed, but worth the effort.

"It's sad," Jamie remarks, "that we can't *all* participate in family activities simultaneously. It has to be splinters of family, pairs. We each have relationships that work independently. But, when we try to join them into a family, we get trouble. So, Brit and I branch off and take aerobics classes together. Or we shop. We diet and bet each other who can lose five pounds first. We both worked hard to build our relationship, so I'm sure it's for keeps. Brittany has become a valued part of my life."

Twisted Arms

While some husbands limit or even prevent relationships between stepmothers and stepchildren, others create the opposite problem. These husbands want stepmothers to become *more* involved than they comfortably can, pressuring them to act as mothers and to usurp the ex-wives' roles in the families. Not surprisingly, these stepmothers encounter strong resistance from their stepchildren whenever they obey their husbands' wishes and attempt to "mother" too much.

"Whenever my stepdaughter Tina visits," Maxine James declares, "my entire daily life is disrupted. My husband pressures me to treat her as if she were my *own* child, but Tina resents *any* parental authority on my part. She tells me, 'I don't have to listen to *you*. I only have to listen to my mother and father.' Tina defies me, Gordon pushes me, and *nobody* considers how *I* feel or what *I* want out of the relationship."

When husbands push stepmothers to act as if they were their stepchildren's *mothers*, stepmothers often feel forced into an unspoken, unwilling rivalry with the children's real mothers. This rivalry is difficult, even when the stepmother agrees that her stepchildren would benefit from a more positive "mother" figure than their real mother provides.

"Tina's mother is both unreliable and undependable. She's moved eight times and changed jobs five times in the last four years. She has affairs with married men and tells Tina, eleven-year-old Tina, all about them. She disappoints Tina all the time. Tells her she'll take her somewhere—the movies, the circus, whatever—and then simply forgets about it. Tina never knows what to expect from her.

"I want to be Tina's role model. I want to show her that it's possible to be a happy, competent woman in a successful marriage. I try to counteract her mother's influence by being dependable and steady. And I know that I've been somewhat successful in providing a comfortable, stable environment for her. She seems relieved, sometimes, when she arrives for visits. Unlike her mother, I keep food in the refrigerator. We have regular meals. We wash dishes. We don't have strangers sleeping over. Tina knows what to expect when she's here."

Even when their stepchildren's mothers *are* stable, however, stepmothers in Maxine's position feel they must measure up to them in their stepchildren's estimations. "I find myself doing things that my stepdaughter's mother might do, trying to get through to her. I invited her to the ballet because I know her mother likes the ballet. Personally, I don't care much for the ballet, but I feel that I have to appeal to my stepchild's—or her mother's—tastes."

Many of these women are particularly frustrated because, left to their own, without pressures from their spouses, they believe they could eventually build decent relationships with their stepchildren. "The point is, I *want* to be close to Tina. But in *my* way, not Gordon's. In *my* time, not his. And, if she rejects me, I want to be able to walk away and say, 'Okay. Let me know if you change your mind.' But my husband won't allow that. He insists that I treat Tina the same way, give her the same attention and affection, that I give our daughter. He won't even consider any other alternatives."

Stepmothers like Maxine lack the authority to *limit* their relationships with their stepchildren because their husbands so intensely want them to replace their ex-wives and recreate their former families. The husbands, determined to offer their children "whole" families, cannot relax and let relationships evolve on their own. And the stepchildren, torn between mother and father and between mother and stepmother, are both unable and unwilling to diminish their loyalties to their mothers in any way, even when their mothers are unstable or neglectful.

This is a situation that often makes stepmothers feel trapped. They are unable to communicate with their husbands, end the competition with their stepchildren's mothers or build satisfying relationships with their stepchildren. Yet most of them continue to try. Like Maxine, they maintain the hope that, someday, if they repeat themselves often enough and gently enough, their husbands will hear their messages. They try to help their husbands see that they do not *have* to replace their former families, that the children neither want nor expect that. And they persist in trying to show their stepchildren that the relationship they offer is in addition to, not instead of, their mothers'. Most admit to frustration and exhaustion and say that they want to limit the levels of their involvement. Nevertheless, they remain committed to their goals of unifying their families.

Against Small Armies

Some women who have no authority with their stepchildren blame not their husbands but their stepchildren's mothers. Their husbands' ex-wives prevent them from participating in their stepchildren's activities so that, ironically, their daily lives are dominated by the *absence* of their stepchildren, rather than by their presence.

Some mothers blame stepmothers for their divorces; others focus their frustrations, whether from divorce, child-rearing, careers or *anything*, onto their ex-husbands' new wives. Many stepchildren imitate their mothers' hostility by rejecting their stepmothers and are rewarded for that rejection by their mothers.

Mia Jordan says that her husband's ex-wife, Kate, focused her rage and spousal jealousy onto Mia, convincing her stepchildren to exclude her from their lives. Six years into her marriage, Mia doesn't participate at all in her stepchildren's visits. Her husband sees his children, Nick and Amy, alone; they haven't seen their half sister, Tracey, in two years and have never even met their half brother, Ben, who is thirteen months old.

"When they were visiting us," Mia sighs, "all our activities centered around Nick and Amy. But no matter how I tried, I could not please them—not with special projects, treats, toys or outings. Nick and Amy resisted me, plain and simple.

"I know, now, that their mother encouraged them to reject me. Kate instructed them carefully about what they could and could not do or discuss with us. After each visit, she questioned them about what had occurred. She bad-mouthed me, but I never knew exactly what she said, so I couldn't defend myself. But no matter what I said or did, the kids didn't *want* to like me. And so, gradually, I admitted defeat. I gave up."

Stepmothers like Mia often feel that their stepchildren are surrounded by an impenetrable barrier set up by the children's mothers. They have no credibility with their stepchildren because the mothers have so thoroughly prejudiced the children against them. They feel misinterpreted and unable to be perceived or taken at face value.

Many of these women initially approached their stepchildren sympathetically, understanding that children of divorce may yearn for their parents to reunite and blame their stepparents for preventing that reunion. However, stepmothers who learn that their stepchildren's mothers have deliberately encouraged or even *created* that blame, tend to become somewhat less sympathetic.

Some mothers try to prevent *any* contact at all between their children and stepmothers. "About three years ago," Mia recalls, "Kate told Nick he should ask his father for 'time alone.' Bob and I both thought this was legitimate. Nick was a preteenage boy with a sister and a half sister, and we thought he could use some time with his dad sans females. But it turned out that what he was asking for was not time alone with Bob, but merely time without *me*. He wanted to be with his sister and his dad, and to reunite as many pieces of his former family as possible."

Sometimes, the mothers of stepchildren seek to drive wedges between stepmothers and their husbands, even when there is no possibility of reconciliation for their former marriages. Because Mia believed that her stepchildren legitimately needed time to "heal" alone with their father, she overlooked Kate's manipulations and agreed to "disappear" for extensive segments of her stepchildren's visits. In retrospect, she says that it was a mistake for her to leave during visits, because that gave Nick, Amy *and* Kate the impression that they could run her out of her home and encouraged their hope that, someday, she might disappear altogether. By leaving, Mia contributed to their sense of power, as well as to their illusion that she and her husband *could* be separated.

"This pattern, in which Tracey and I left when Nick and Amy arrived, continued for some time. The result was that I became incredibly self-conscious in my own home. I watched for signs of Nick and Amy's contentment or resentment. I monitored conversations, to see if I should enter them or not. I walked on eggshells. I laid low. My husband was torn, unable to please anyone. And we had no idea if they were any happier."

Interference by the stepchildren's mothers has led some stepfamilies to court battles over visitation. Some fathers accuse their ex-wives of obstructing visitation; others simply try to clarify and enforce existing agreements. A few attempt to acquire physical custody of their children, claiming that their children's mothers have deliberately alienated their affections. However, most of the time, court orders provide little help, since they are difficult to enforce and, once enforced, can simply aggravate existing problems.

When Bob eventually took Kate to court to enforce his visitation rights, the court upheld Bob's unconditional right to see his children without Mia having to leave home, but the decision didn't accomplish anything. Nick stood up and told the court, "You can make me visit him, but you can't make me like it! You can't make me *love* him!"

Although most stepmothers know that the divisions in the family are not their fault and that they have done nothing wrong, many feel guilt or sorrow at being the focal point of family hostilities. They feel sorry for their husbands, themselves, their children and their stepchildren, all of whom are victims of the animosities of the children's mothers. A few said they tried to talk about family dynamics with their husbands' ex-wives, but came to believe that, when the ex-wives learned how upset they were making their husbands, they became triumphant rather than concerned. Others, feeling powerless and frustrated, simply backed off, abandoning relationships with their stepchildren entirely.

"One day," says Mia, "I just let go. I let go of the part of Bob that belongs to those kids. I let go of my idea of 'family,' of wanting to be part of my stepchildren's lives, and of wanting my kids and my stepkids to have relationships. I took myself out of the picture, and told

Bob to salvage what he could of his relationship with Nick and Amy, because it was costing him too dearly to cling to an ideal that the kids didn't share. I suggested that they get together, just the three of them, without me or Tracey or Ben. And they do see each other, occasionally, that way."

Not all of the stepmothers in this kind of situation allow their stepchildren's mothers to completely block their authority or cut off contact with the children. But their participation in their stepchildren's lives is dominated and orchestrated by the children's mother, who employs her children as convenient vessels of hostility for their father. As a result, some stepchildren learn to play one parent's anger against the other, manipulating situations to their advantage and acquiring substantial powers of their own.

In Mia's family, the balance of power has become completely askew. "Bob has no say at all about Nick and Amy anymore. No one seems to see that *he's* the father and that *they* are the kids. They, through their mother, hold all the power."

Unable to resolve the power struggles with their stepchildren's mothers, stepmothers like Mia try to drop out and abdicate their roles. However, most find that escape is not so easy; daily life continues to be affected by their estranged stepchildren.

"They haunt me," declares Mia. "They taunt us with their absence. We feel them with us, in that our baby looks like Nick, and in that four-year-old Tracey cries because she misses them. When they visited us, they disrupted our daily lives. Now that they don't visit, our routines are uninterrupted, but their daily impact is more disruptive, more destructive, than ever."

With Arms Extended

"My stepson's problems are so pervasive, his needs are so extensive," one stepmother states, "that it's hard to find a moment in time or a corner of space that doesn't include him."

Stepmothers whose stepchildren are "severely troubled" have difficulty defining personal territory because their lives and their stepchildren's are so intermingled. These women, whose stepchildren's problems include drug or alcohol abuse, sexual promiscuity, repeated truancy and failure at school, habitual shoplifting and attempted suicide, focus their attention so heavily on their stepchildren that their personal time and space all but disappear. Nonetheless, most remain committed to helping their stepchildren and freely give of their love, time and patience. Many participate in family therapy.

Most of these stepmothers feel that the importance of their own goals or problems pales in light of their stepchildren's urgent needs. They put their own interests aside to try to help their families resolve their crises. As newcomers to their families, they often adopt roles of impartial observers to family interactions, seeing themselves as "middlemen," "buffers," "umpires" or "interpreters." Often, these are exhausting roles. Sometimes they lead to conflicts with other family members. Generally, they are without reward.

Jill Sterling's stepson, Charlie, tried to hang himself after becoming despondent during his parents' custody fight.

"We've all been in therapy together since then," Jill says. "Charlie, his parents and me. We're all very involved in each others' lives. I talk to Charlie's mother, Ellen, on the phone at least once a day. I discuss Charlie with my husband and update him on Ellen's comments constantly. I try to buffer their mutual blame, dispel their suspicions of each other, minimize their guilt. I'm the cushion, in a way, that softens the impact of their emotional upheaval. I'm a comparatively neutral link between them and Charlie. The three of us analyze, criticize, talk and argue, and usually I'm the referee. All three of us, though, are consumed by Charlie and are forever putting our own desires, problems and emotions aside to help him."

Jill recalled how violently the family was shocked by Charlie's suicide attempt. "We were stunned. Horrified. For reassurance, or out of helpless confusion, we rallied and clung together. For months, we were on a 'suicide watch.' We *never* left Charlie alone. We monitored what he said, whether and how much he talked about death or suicide, poison or guns. We watched what he ate and drank. We clued his teachers in. We were obsessed with Charlie, his well-being, his survival.

"Well, he's survived, so far. It's been over a year. He knows we care. We've seen him through every twist and turn his problems have taken. But my little kids, Beth and Billy, have been overlooked, by comparison. And so has my marriage. And so have I. I'm worn out. And, at a more and more conscious level, I resent the fact that, because *we* don't have crises all the time, the rest of us get forgotten. In a bizarre way, I think Charlie controls us with his problems. He keeps the entire family hopping around him."

Stepmothers whose stepchildren have problems as severe as Charlie's often describe parents and siblings as "devastated," "paralyzed" and "heartbroken." They say that the effects on their own lives are no less sweeping, but that they have found, like Jill, that they *must* step in to provide much-needed objectivity and level-headedness that are beyond the others involved. These stepmothers are able to step back and take a hard look at the needs of the *entire* family, so that adjustments can be made without everyone succumbing to grief and concern. What Jill saw from her perspective allowed her to help family members steady themselves, acknowledge their personal limits and begin to structure the time and the attention they pay to Charlie, without blame or guilt.

"We were treating Charlie's problems like a two-year-old's tantrums. If you give the child attention every time he has one, you encourage the tantrums. When we ran obsessively to Charlie's assistance with our undivided attention, we weren't necessarily helping him. We were rewarding him for having problems, and we were neglecting ourselves."

If stepmothers of disturbed, intensely angry or self-destructive children are to help their stepchildren effectively, they must also take care of themselves and the other family members. No matter how involved they are with their stepchildren, they must maintain some separate personal time and territory, and must have the authority to set their own limits. Like Jill, they must remember not to let themselves be swept away by their stepchildren's problems. "At one point," Jill explains, "I crossed some kind of emotional threshold. I regained some kind of emotional distance and control. Despite all the chaos in our family, I realized that I still have two small children to raise, a husband to love, my own life to live and *some* personal needs that have to be respected. I care about Charlie, and I'm determined to help him, but there are limits: I won't sink, or let our family sink, to help him swim."

Arm Wrestling

Even though they are grown, adult stepchildren often have a profound impact on their stepmothers' daily lives. Their stepmothers often wish they had more authority, but find that their stepchildren are too old to be controlled by their parents, let alone by stepparents. And, age aside, many stepmothers aren't sure that their roles *should* encompass discipline or limit setting.

Most stepmothers who share respect, values and similar lifestyles with their grown stepchildren find that their stepfamilies achieve a degree of peace and harmony. However, for the majority of the women we interviewed, such is not the case. They complained that their stepchildren's moral standards are weak and their self-images distorted; that, among other failings, their stepchildren are selfish, self-centered, immature, materialistic, destructive, manipulative and ungrateful. Their stepchildren, according to over half of these stepmothers, are "cases of arrested development" or "too lazy to take out the trash, let alone take responsibility for their own lives." And many said that, even as adults, stepchildren continue to blame their problems or failures on their parents' divorces, perpetually expecting their parents to solve problems or bail them out of trouble.

Marla Jenson finds little in common with either of her two adult stepchildren, Eric and Tiffany, and holds little hope of establishing close relationships with them, even after eight years of marriage. "Their values, morals and ideas about how to conduct their lives and treat other people have long since been established," Marla explains. "They see life differently than I do. And, really, it isn't my place to impose my views on them. It was their parents' job to instill those things. I'm not their mother. Besides, it's way too late to change them, anyway."

Stepmothers like Marla complain that they often feel used or taken advantage of by their stepchildren. Many of their stepchildren, although grown and working, still accept hefty financial assistance from their fathers. Some depend on their parents completely, living with them or receiving full financial support.

Stepmothers facing this family dynamic believe their husbands are being manipulated by their stepchildren and are unable to resist the manipulation for a variety of reasons. Some men fear abandonment by their adult children; others want to compensate for the breakup of their children's home; a few actually hope to buy their children's love.

"Eric's game—and I do believe it is a game," Marla explains, "is to blame his father for ruining his life. In order to prove that his life is ruined, he'll do *anything*. I know he was hurt by his parents' divorce. But Eric has simply found the perfect way to avoid growing up. It's easier to cry 'hurt' and let Daddy support him than it is to write papers, work and take exams."

Like Marla, most stepmothers are unable to change their step-children, their husbands or the patterns between them. They can neither persuade their stepchildren to let go nor assure their husbands that their children will love them even without open invitations, endless gifts and unlimited funds. Eventually, realizing that they can't change *others*, some decide to change *themselves*.

"I got fed up," says Marla. "The sorry truth is that my step-children's parents failed to instill values. I'd like to compensate for this and teach Eric and Tiffany right from wrong, but I can't. Yet I can't stand by passively, either. So, what I do—all I *can* do—is stake out *my* turf, and insist that on *my* turf you follow *my* rules."

In order to protect their marriages, property and self-respect, women like Marla establish territorial limits and declare authority in their own domains. "I don't allow Tiffany to use my home as her flopping ground any more. She needs to ask me if she wants to sleep here. And, if she eats a meal here, she's expected to help. Same with Eric. It took years and a screaming showdown or two, but they know, now, not to mess with me on my turf."

For many stepmothers, confrontational, emotional scenes are unavoidable if they are to assert themselves in the family. Unable to work as teams with their husbands, they must speak up on their own if they are to maintain their self-respect. Those who do this, however, soon realize that the scope of their control is limited.

"Outside the home," Marla sighs, "I have no influence over what goes on between Steve and my stepchildren. If Steve wants to buy them expensive toys, I can't stop him. But I *can* put his extravagance into perspective for him. Last spring, I stopped wasting energy getting angry and started to look after my own interests. Instead of getting upset when Tiffany persuaded Steve to get her a phone for the new car he'd bought her, I got myself a car phone, too. I simply drove my four-year-old car into a dealership and bought a new car that came with a phone. I showed Steve my new car phone when he came home from work that evening. He understood instantly how things were going to be. And I've made sure he continues to understand. When he gave Tiffany three hundred dollars for new clothes, I deposited an equal amount in our daughter's bank account and spent five hundred dollars on a new designer suit for myself!"

At first, Marla felt foolish following this routine. But she's found it has been a more effective means of communication than any verbal exchange. "Steve is actually *learning* from this. On the surface, he's learning that whatever he spends on them, I'll spend as much or more on me or our daughter. But he's also noticing how often he does things for them, how much it costs, how little it accomplishes. He's beginning to feel used. He's told Eric that this is the last tuition *or* rent he'll pay unless Eric finishes the semester. He's told Tiffany that she'll have to pay her own rent starting with the next lease renewal. He's wising up."

Some stepmothers with adult stepchildren did report comfortable, friendly relationships. Those who did not, however, said they find some success in maintaining equilibrium when they take control of their own homes and define their own authority. Those who achieve the most satisfaction are stepmothers who limit their goals, accept other family members and their relationships as they are, protect their own children and interests, and declare their own rules on their own territory. "I deal with it the only way I can," Marla explains. "I look after my own. And I look away from the rest."

Strong Arm

When their stepchildren live with them, most stepmothers find that their daily lives are dominated by their participation in stepchildren's activities. Many struggle to establish even small traces of personal territory. Further, whether they want to or not, whether their husbands encourage them or not, whether their stepchildren resist them or not, these women feel that, simply as one of the two adults in the home, they must maintain authoritative roles.

Some stepmothers whose stepchildren live with them have taken on more authority than they are comfortable with. Maggie Joyner constantly wrestles with the prerogative of authority. "I've struggled from day one with the limits of my right to discipline Josh. As an adult, I knew I should have some say over his behavior in my home, but I really didn't want it. I wanted his mother and father to take responsibility for his discipline. They didn't. So, the choice I had was to take on more authority than I was comfortable with or to let Josh be neglected, with no rules to guide him and no one to hold him accountable. It became my job, by default, to set Josh's limits and hold him to them."

Stepmothers like Maggie often blame the parents for their step-children's trouble, and say that their husbands seem incapable of enforcing discipline or rules. They have difficulty defining the parameters of their roles and feel entangled in the residual conflicts of their husbands' former marriages. In order to help create structure for their stepchildren, they become more involved than they want to, sometimes stepping into old battles between ex-spouses.

Maggie believes that her husband Brad and his ex-wife, Maria, are often more interested in blaming each other for their son's problems than in helping him. "It's taken us *years* in family therapy to see what's happened," Maggie says. "But their parenting, when they were together, reflected the problems of their marriage, and Josh got lost in that conflict. They both became 'enablers.' They allowed Josh to misbehave and didn't hold him accountable, even when he drove the car without a license and had an accident, even when he went to school stoned and got suspended. And so, I felt I *had* to step in."

For stepmothers like Maggie, asserting authority is necessary for their own survival in the family. The limits they set and enforce are not only for their stepchildrens' benefits, but for their own. One of the most common areas of concern is personal space. "I was sharing my kitchen, living room and bathroom, not only with a new husband, but with a teenage boy. I needed *some* things to be *mine*," Maggie explains. "And I needed Josh to realize that, even if his dad didn't care what he borrowed or used, *I* did, and I was somebody separate, not just an appendage of Brad.

"I taught Josh to ask before he took things, but it was difficult. I had to be quite explicit about what was 'mine,' 'ours' or 'his.' We labeled things with our names. For a while, we actually labeled food in the refrigerator if we wanted to save it. I had to laugh when Josh's mother called to complain that, when he visited her, he'd put his name on leftover cartons of chop suey. I knew, then, that it was finally sinking in that there were boundaries between people, and that Josh knew that he, that all of us, could have private space, possessions and respect. And that meant I might not find my chicken legs gone anymore when I went to get my lunch."

Although many of these women have had tremendous success in setting limits and enforcing discipline, they are uncomfortable about their roles. Unsure not only of what their roles *should* be, but also of what they *want* them to be, they often express resentment that the parents are not more responsible, relieving them of the *need* to take on so much authority.

"Josh was positively hungry for limits," Maggie told us. "Once he understood that they were consistent, he grabbed onto my rules. But I constantly weigh what's legitimately my role versus Josh's parents' roles. Unfortunately, the definitions are irrelevant most of the time, because situations call for me to *act*, whether or not the action is theoretically appropriate to 'my' role. For example, when Josh's drug problems got too big for us to deal with by ourselves, *I* was the one who insisted that he go into a residential rehab. His parents couldn't make that decision. I had to fight Brad, Maria and Josh on that one. So far, it's proved to be the right decision. But, at the time, who knew if I was right? Or if it was my place to push his parents around?"

Stepmothers in similar situations feel that *all* the family members—their stepchildren, their husbands and their husbands' ex-wives—depend on them for structure, stability and limits. They may give more than they had intended or, sometimes, imagined possible, but most of them feel needed, important and powerful. However, like Maggie, many are uncomfortable with the degree of power and authority they hold. "It's as if the parents have simply quit," one stepmother remarked, "and dumped all the parenting onto me."

Heavily Armed

Even when their husbands are strong authority figures, heavily involved in parenting and discipline, stepmothers whose stepchildren live with them often need to establish and maintain clear authority on their own. They have to assert themselves independently of the strong father figure and clarify their roles in the family hierarchy, both for their stepchildren and for themselves.

Julie Sinclair remembers the first few weeks of living with her stepchildren as completely frantic, without time to consider her role, much less her status in the family. "The entire structure of my life disintegrated when my stepchildren moved in. Car pools, dentists, PTA meetings—all the activities that come with having three children—completely swallowed me up. Privacy, even the *thought* of privacy, was a thing of the past. No conversation went uninterrupted. No scheduled activity, not even my work, was exempt from cancellation in order to accommodate the kids. My life, as I had known it, was run over by a steamroller named Zach-Kevin-Tori, and I was reeling, trying to get some sense of balance in my life."

Julie remembers that this frantic pace continued for about six weeks, until Trevor announced that he had to go out of town for a few days. Julie panicked. "The kids and I had no dynamic from which to work alone. Our relationship had revolved around Trevor, their dad, my husband."

Many stepmothers like Julie remember beginning their stepmother relationships as "Dad's assistant." Their husbands brought everyone together and remained the central, focal figures in their stepfamilies, the clear leaders from whom everyone took signals. Although many stepmothers are comfortable with this dynamic, they find that it has disadvantages.

Julie explains, "I was glad to *remain* Trevor's assistant. But then Trevor had to leave town on business, and my relationship with the kids was undefined, untested. Nobody, neither they nor I, had any idea of how to operate. We were all still getting used to each other. The pecking order wasn't clear. And Trevor was leaving. I felt like I was drowning."

Situations like Julie's are often resolved through confrontations. Julie's relationships with the children really began while Trevor was away. "I remember an atmosphere of tension and uncertainty, as if everyone was waiting to see what would happen without Trevor around. On the second night, we found out.

"The children simply refused to go to bed. They challenged me while eating bedtime snacks. I vividly remember the cream-filled donuts and milk, and trying to get the kids to finish up quickly while they tried to drag things out. Zach challenged me, finally. 'I'm not going to bed and you can't make me,' he announced. And then, staring into my eyes, he chewed his donut in exaggerated slow motion."

What happened next surprised even Julie. In the context of stress and uncertainty, Zach's comment began a chain reaction within her that she still finds difficult to comprehend.

"I yanked Zachary up out of his chair, pushed him against the wall and proceeded to dump six weeks of fury onto him. 'Who do you think you are?' I screamed at him. I don't even know what else I said. I just let out all my frustrations, tensions and exhaustion. I shrieked at

Zach to get upstairs and then I turned to Kevin. He didn't move fast enough, so I *pushed* him up the stairs, telling them both that I didn't want to hear another *word*. With the maddening cleverness of childhood they didn't *speak* another word, but hurried up the stairs making animal noises.

"I followed them into their room, where I launched into a tirade about the sacrifices I'd made and would forever be making for them. I told them that they didn't have to love me or even *like* me but that we *did* have to get along. When I left, I was shaking and tears were running down my face, and I knew, instinctively, that they should not see me crying.

"I stood, sobbing, outside their door, and I heard them discussing me. Their comments were amazing! 'She's not so bad,' and 'I think she likes us,' and things like that. After I'd calmed down, I went back in to say goodnight. Kevin put his arms around me and said he loved me. Zach told me he was glad I lived with them."

That night marked the beginning of Julie's "family." Although she regrets that she lost control and is far from proud of her display of anger, she believes that her outburst gave her status, proved her to be powerful and demonstrated to the children that she cared. The children accepted her authority.

Although they don't all explode like Julie, many stepmothers believe that some sort of shared emotional release is necessary before stepchildren, stepmother and father can begin to meld into a "family." Until such a release occurs, tensions and questions build without anyone knowing how to express *any* emotion, whether affection or anger. "I'd been looking for signs of caring and appreciation from them, and they'd been searching for similar signals from me," Julie recalls. "It wasn't that we danced this dance on purpose. It was that nobody knew how to take the first step. My outburst, while it didn't express emotion gently, broke the ice, opening the way for other feelings, including affection, to come out.

In addition to allowing emotional expression, many stepmothers need to exhibit well-defined, authoritative power early in their relationships with their stepchildren. By doing so, they eliminate much of the endless introspection and internal conflicts that plague them. Even stepmothers like Julie, however, are certain that they never completely solve all the authority problems presented by their stepchildren. Adult authority and the ability to discipline are constantly tested by children and stepchildren of all ages. For some stepmothers, such testing is actually a mark of their firm establishment in the family; they are challenged because they are one of the adults in the home, not because they are stepmothers.

Daily Life

Stepmothers unanimously find that their stepchildren have a profound effect on their daily lives. This is true regardless of factors like visitation schedules, physical custody, the stepchildren's ages and the presence or absence of stepsiblings.

It's as true for Jessie and Mia, who never even see their stepchildren, as it is for Julie and Maggie, whose stepchildren live with them.

It's as true for Maggie, Julie and Molly, whose husbands encourage their independent relationships with their stepchildren, as it is for Jennifer and Jamie, whose husbands try to minimize or control all contact.

It's true for Marla, who feels she must protect her husband from his children, and for Maxine, who feels she must protect herself and her stepchild from her husband's demands.

Among stepmothers whose main daily issue is authority, some, like Maggie, have too much; others, like Jennifer, have none. Still others, like Julie and Marla, have virtually been cornered into establishing the level of authority they want.

Differences also exist among those stepmothers whose greatest daily issue is their stepchildren's activities. Like Jill, some find themselves drowning in their stepchildren's affairs; others, like Mia, find themselves totally excluded.

With respect to personal territory, some stepmothers, like Jessie, want to banish their stepchildren; others, like Molly, welcome them unconditionally.

Regardless of the issues that most affect stepmothers' everyday routines, those who are happiest are those who, without trying to change anyone else, decide what sort of daily role they want with their stepchildren and balance that decision against the needs of the other family members. These women approach the role with a positive attitude, they exhibit great flexibility and they are willing to work at the relationship, no matter what it takes.

Advice From Stepmothers on Day-to-Day Issues

1.   **Know how much authority, personal territory and participation you want in the children's activities.** Decide what you need and how flexible you can be. Decide what compromises you can comfortably make. Don't compromise to the extent that you sacrifice your happiness. Don't allow yourself to be devoured by the needs or demands of your stepchildren.

2.   **Communicate with your husband.** Make sure you and your husband share goals and agree on the scope of your relationship with your stepchildren. Make sure he'll back up your right to authority and personal territory, and that he'll support your decisions about how involved you *want* to be with his children.

3.   **Be a team with your husband.** Make sure you support and reinforce each other on a daily basis. Don't let the children play one of you against the other; don't let your husband play you against the children. Be sure you and he understand what the other wants from the marriage, and that you have a shared concept of how his children fit into that framework.

4.   **Don't try to be a savior.** Tackle what is reasonable; set realistic goals for yourself and your stepchildren. If there are problems, remember the adage: Change what you can, don't try to change what you can't, and have the wisdom to know the difference. Realize you will never have as much impact as the children's mother, and be as consistent as possible with her and your husband in your goals for your stepchildren. Don't try to usurp or infringe upon the territory of the parents. And make sure you preserve your own privacy and personal space.

5.   **Be available.** Offer choices to your stepchildren; let them decide how close or how distant they want the relationship to be. But welcome them, and let them know you are willing to be close. Express your interest in them and your affection for them, and show them you have room for them on your daily agenda.

6.   **Be prepared to handle rejection.** Be open to relationships with your stepchildren, but try not to invest any more than you can afford to lose. Remember that those relationships are a risk. Don't depend on them—and don't let the happiness or success of your family depend on them, either.

7.   **Be aware of who has how much power.** Be careful what you reinforce on a daily basis. By paying extra attention to stepchildren because they're acting negatively, you may be encouraging that negative behavior and allowing them the power to control the family through negative displays.

8.   **Accept your right to authority and personal territory.** Simply because you are one of the adults in the family, it's part of your job to have authority and to add your influence to the parenting team. Give what you can to your stepchildren, and let them know your requirements, such as respect for your authority and some personal privacy or space.

9.   **Be flexible.** Any time you're dealing with more than one person, you've got to expect the unexpected and be ready for unpredictable changes in plans. When the people you're dealing with are children, that's even more true. And when they are *step*children— with their mother, father, and sometimes, stepfather, *and* you involved in their plans—it's even truer!

10.   **Be patient.** It may take a long time to balance everybody's needs on a daily basis. Don't expect yourself to fix everything for everybody all the time. Give your family time to develop and grow together. Most of all, relax.

FOUR

Legal and Material Issues

Stepmothers face difficulties with many legal and material issues, the most problematic being finances, custody and visitation, and wills.

Finances are challenging for many stepmothers because the child support costs their husbands must pay are constantly escalating. Whether their assets are held jointly with their husbands or independently, these women have difficulty planning their own finances because they can neither anticipate nor estimate these recurring increases. Others do not mind the actual court-ordered support; it's the unexpected expenses, both large and small, that aggravate them. Some stepmothers find that their own lifestyles have suffered significantly due to the costs incurred by their stepchildren. Others allege that their stepchildren's mothers use money either as revenge or as hooks with which to hang on to their ex-husbands.

Some stepmothers who are also mothers feel the need to protect their own children's financial interests from those of their stepchildren. Others see their own personal assets as endangered by their husbands' generosity to their stepchildren. Some carefully keep track of all expenses related to their stepchildren; others prefer not to know what's being spent. While many are glad to spend whatever their

67

stepchildren need, most of the women we interviewed stated that they never anticipated how extensive that spending would be.

Stepmothers who have problems concerning visitation and custody range from those who have physical custody to those who never see their stepchildren at all. Visitation plagues women who welcome their stepchildren's visits as well as those who dread them. Some women complain that their marriages, or even their husbands' personalities, change dramatically during visits; most say that visits disrupt their normally peaceful homes. Some whose stepchildren live with them are upset by the upheaval that accompanies visits with the stepchildren's mothers. Others find that ongoing parental battles about visitation or custody destroy their own and their stepchildren's peace of mind.

Wills and estate planning are particularly difficult for most stepmothers. To avoid dealing with the complexities of multilayered property distribution, a number of stepmothers have written wills that simply leave everything to their husbands. Others have composed amazingly complicated documents that involve trusts, denominated savings accounts and convoluted conditions of inheritance for beneficiaries and alternates. Many stepmothers find the subject of their estates so tangled that they have postponed will writing indefinitely. Others diminish the importance of their wills by maintaining bank accounts in their children's names or establishing trust funds for each child.

The reasons wills are problematic for stepmothers vary with their situations. Women who brought children to the marriage often want their wills to separate their children's inheritances from those of their stepchildren. Women with children from their present marriage often want their wills to divide the marital estate in favor of their natural children. They worry that if they name their husbands as their beneficiaries their personal assets may be passed, through their husbands, to their stepchildren rather than to their biological children.

In the course of writing their wills, stepmothers confront their deepest feelings about family loyalty and responsibility. Some want to give their stepchildren and their own children an equal inheritance; others seek to give each child what that child *needs*, without concern for what the others receive. Some agree with their husbands about their joint estates, but many cannot find common ground, and about a third say they are dissatisfied with the terms to which they have agreed.

Almost every stepmother has difficulty with finances, visitation or wills. Most find that their difficulties with one issue lead to or involve difficulties with others, so much so that it is often difficult to distinguish one issue from another.

Sharing the Wealth

A few stepmothers say that they are not bothered by any legal or material issues regarding their stepchildren. Most of these women have no children of their own and are married to wealthy or "financially comfortable" men. They welcome their stepchildren to visit as much as they want, encourage their husbands to give even more financial support than they are required to pay, and make sure that both their own and their husbands' wills provide amply for their stepchildren. If these women have a gripe, it's not about their stepchildren; it's about their stepchildren's mothers.

Molly Jerome married forty-six-year-old Ed, owner of a successful industrial supply business, five years ago. Molly's complaint is that Ed's ex-wife continually asks for more money and favors beyond what Ed is obligated to pay. "She's jealous of Ed's financial security and even more jealous that Ed's married to somebody else. Even though she has remarried, it's clear that she isn't emotionally finished with Ed. Money is one way she can hold on to him. Money, and making arrangements for the boys to visit."

Many stepmothers without children of their own are comfortable leaving the bulk of their marital estates to their stepchildren. Often, their only concern regarding their stepchildren and money is seeing that their stepchildren have enough. "I want to make sure that they always have more than they need," Molly comments. "That's partly because I never want to be accused of standing between them and their father's money, or of taking from them what they feel should be theirs. I'm always reminding Ed to invest money for them, or to make deposits in their accounts. Neither of them will ever have cause to complain about their finances."

Some stepmothers whose husbands have substantial financial assets are concerned that their stepchildren and other family members suspect that they married their husbands for their money. Like Molly, they feel defensive and go out of their way to dispel this suspicion, even if it means spending excessively on their stepchildren.

"I married Ed because I love him. His companionship, his *life*, is what I want to share. His money makes our life easier and more comfortable than it otherwise might have been, but I'd like to think that I'd have married him even if he were broke. I believe that, when he's gone, his money should pass to his children. I know that, if I outlive him, he'll make sure that I have everything I need as long as I live. But I don't want the boys, or their mother, or anybody else to think that I took anything from his children. If I change the estate at all, it will be by adding to their inheritance, not by taking away."

Nickels, Dimes and Wealthy Stepmothers

If finances in general, including wills, do not affect couples like Molly and Ed Jerome, they cause major differences of opinion for many others. Stepmothers with children are often faced with the problem of protecting their own children's financial interests without favoring them over their stepchildren. And, for stepmothers whose assets exceed their husbands', there is often difficulty not only in deciding what to spend on each child, but also in deciding how to divide their estate fairly in their wills.

Dentist Maxine James's major financial problem as a stepmother is estate planning. "My family is sound, financially," she says. "My father built a metals business from scratch, or I should say, scrap, and sold it for a small fortune. When my daughter, Ruthie, was born, my father set up a trust fund for her. Money generated by that trust will pay for her college tuition and grad school, if she wants. There will be money for her to set up a business, buy a house and live quite well.

"Neither Gordon's parents nor his ex-wife's are able to provide anything like that for my stepdaughter, Tina. She has no trust fund or any other financial guarantees for the future. Gordon is troubled because he sees a huge inequality in the finances of his two children. We can't agree on a will because Gordon firmly believes that one hundred percent of *our* assets should go to Tina, to compensate for these financial differences."

When the financial assets of their children vastly exceed those of their stepchildren, stepmothers find that major tensions in their marriages can result. Some husbands want to equalize their children's finances, no matter what it requires. Stepmothers, however, usually oppose such measures. They see no reason why their children and their stepchildren should have equal assets, especially if it would mean that some of *their* personal property would pass to their stepchildren, rather than to their own.

"Gordon believes," Maxine complains, "that since Ruthie won't need our money, it should all go to *his* child. He wants me to leave everything to him when I die, so that he can leave it all to Tina. If he dies first, he wants me to promise that I'll leave whatever I don't need to Tina. But I don't want to leave *anything* to Tina, other than a portion of Gordon's share of our joint assets. I don't think that what my parents have done for their granddaughter has *anything* to do with Tina, any more than it does with any other child who is not their granddaughter. I don't mean to leave Tina in the cold like a starving match girl, but I don't want to work and build an estate for her, either. Not when I have a child of my own. And especially not when the relationship I have with Tina is so frustrating!"

Because their ideas are so far apart, couples like Maxine and Gordon rarely even discuss their wills, much less reach compromises. Stepmothers like Maxine are reluctant to make their children sacrifice for the sake of their stepchildren, and feel torn between their husbands' wishes and their own children's interests. Because each parent is motivated by the basic desire to take care of his or her children, neither is likely to back down or compromise. Their standoffs, however, often enhance competitive feelings between spouses and rivalries between half siblings.

"Gordon is forever comparing what Ruthie has to what Tina has," Maxine says. "He compares not only the big items, like their savings or shares in our real estate, but tiny, insignificant things, as well. And, because he compares things that way, Tina does, too. Ruthie is only three years old, but I have to apologize that she *may* have more dolls than Tina did when *she* was three. And Tina manipulates us, as if we are obligated to make this up to her. The trouble is that Gordon agrees. What's fair for Ruthie is fair for Tina, according to him. We're at a complete dead end."

Although wills and estates are frequently the issue most troubling to stepmothers whose assets exceed their husbands', many women find that they are actually *more* upset by everyday expenses. They feel that their stepchildren constantly try to take financial advantage of them, often in minor, but annoying, ways. Most do not mind spending the money involved as much as they mind the feeling of being used or exploited, even for relatively small sums.

"Gordon pays an extremely generous amount of child support for Tina, and that's fine," Maxine says. "But, even so, we have to pay incredible sums during every visit. It's maddening to me how Gordon and I are endlessly nickled and dimed.

"It's normal for Tina to show up on a Saturday morning and announce that she has a birthday party to attend that afternoon and needs to buy a present and something to wear to the party. So I have to change my plans and hurry off shopping with her. Gordon's monthly payments *should* cover these items. Who knows *what* Tina's mother does with the money he sends—she sure doesn't buy Tina's party clothes! I know I could refuse to run to the mall, but that would make Gordon angry and cause more problems than it's worth."

Complaints like Maxine's are not limited to "rich" stepmothers. Many women with moderate incomes whose husbands pay sufficient child support resent the relatively minor, but extra, expenses of their stepchildren's visits. Like Maxine, many are at least as annoyed by the time they spend and the power plays involved as by the actual expenses involved.

One stepmother lamented that support payments don't take into consideration the costs of stepchildren's weekly visits. "They're with us two days each week, but we pay their mother for seven. That's over a hundred days each year we pay for *twice!*" Each visit, she says, can actually cost hundreds of dollars, because the children expect to eat at restaurants, buy clothes or toys and be entertained.

In most cases, stepmothers attribute the ultimate problem to the definition of family. They and their husbands define family differently and, therefore, see their responsibilities and loyalties differently. "Across the board, Gordon wants the girls to be equal in every way, as if they were sisters. They are *not* sisters. They have different mothers. And I simply cannot feel about Tina the way I feel about my own child, nor can I accept the same degree of responsibility for her upbringing and financial future."

Many stepmothers discover that writing their wills causes them to define their relationships, declare allegiances and clarify their roles. For those like Maxine, loyalty to their children outweighs their desire for harmony with their husbands. The process of writing their wills ultimately requires them to face major issues and draw lines separating their husbands' family goals from their own. Many, faced with difficult decisions, are hesitant to act.

"I know that I *have* to make a will," Maxine declares. "I have to for Ruthie's sake. I know I should get a lawyer and protect whatever assets I can, like my dental practice, certain pieces of jewelry, my pension, things like that. I should, because if I died right now, during this conversation, all my assets would, by law, go to Gordon because I don't have a will, and Gordon would give most of my things to Tina. I don't want my stepdaughter to get my grandmother's engagement ring, but I don't want to go to a lawyer behind my husband's back, either. Yet, if I do it openly, it will create a horrible rift in our marriage. So, without a will, I feel like I'm standing in the middle of the road, hoping that a truck doesn't hit me."

Wills, Plans and Partners

Other stepmothers attack the issue right from the start. "We talked about money management and estate planning up front, before we even got engaged," attorney Jamie Simpkins says. She and her husband, Keith, both in their early forties, avoided a lot of frustrations because they foresaw how certain legal and material issues might affect them. Before they married, they discussed finances, custody and wills at length, in an attempt to plan ahead and minimize future problems.

"It was clear that we'd need to have a method for dealing with expenses and investments for the kids, because each of us had a child from a previous marriage and we knew we wanted to have at least one more child."

Couples like Jamie and Keith discuss the assets they are each bringing to the marriage, what the husband/father will have to pay in child support, and, when applicable, what the wife/mother will receive in support for the children she brings with her. They list their assets and review the anticipated costs of raising each of their children, through college.

Stepmothers like Jamie believe that they should plan for the needs of *all* the family's children, regardless of who the actual parents are. Accordingly, as part of their planning, many open separate investment accounts for each child and budget regular deposits in order to save enough for college or other major expenses.

"I was very touched," Jamie recalls, "when Keith said we shouldn't depend on my ex-husband to put my son Danny through college. Keith was willing to contribute as much as Danny would need. If Frank, Danny's father, comes through, fine, but Keith wants to be sure that Danny gets a good education, even if Frank refuses to contribute. That means a lot to me."

When couples like Jamie and Keith have children together, they adjust their plans to include the new babies. To protect each child's future, they devise methods of saving portions of their earnings for their children. But foreseeing major expenses and dividing assets to prepare for them is not their only financial plan. "Keith and I think that managing money is important, so we give all three children allowances, even though my stepdaughter lives with her mother. The allowances are intended to help them learn to handle money responsibly. Of course, *our* son Stuart gets less than the older kids. He's still so young that his allowance is basically comic-book money, but it teaches him that if he spends it all on candy as soon as he gets it, he won't be able to buy any more candy, or anything else, until the next week."

Many women, like Jamie, share all their assets with their husbands, and each spouse's will usually leaves everything to the other. They believe that, although their husbands might favor their own children emotionally, they can be trusted to look after all the children's financial needs fairly. Most attribute this trust to the common view they share with their husbands of how to handle their money, particularly where stepchildren are concerned.

"Keith and I are almost completely in agreement when it comes to the concept of money. I say 'concept,'" she laughs, "because Keith tends to *act* differently than he *talks*, buying Brittany something whenever she bats her eyelashes at him. But, in *theory*, we both see our money as a resource that's there for what we, as a family, *need*. First, for whatever is essential for our family's survival. Beyond that, once we're all fed, clothed, healthy and educated, *then* it's there for what will enrich us, together or individually. We see the money as a pool or fund not necessarily to be divided equally, but to be drawn upon to help each child do or become what he or she wants to do to or become."

For such women, definitions of family fall easily into place when it comes to wills and finances. "It doesn't matter whose kid it is," Jamie concludes. "Brittany is just as much our responsibility as Danny or Stuart. We're all here to help each other. That's what 'family' is."

Battles of the Wills

Many couples do not have wills because they simply cannot agree on how they want to divide their property. Particularly when there are children from their current marriages, stepmothers and their husbands tend to disagree about what would be fair. Fathers often want all their children to receive equal shares of their estates; stepmothers usually have different ideas.

"I've always felt that, should George or I die while our children are under eighteen, they'd be far more upset than my stepchildren," one stepmother explains. "First of all, my stepchildren are older and can contribute to their own support. One already works part-time. Second, they live with their mother and stepfather, so their home lives would be unchanged by the death of their father or me. Finally, their mother and stepfather both work, so they would not have to rely completely on our estate in the event of our deaths.

"*Our* children, on the other hand, would be devastated by the absence of either of us. And it will be over a decade before either of them is old enough to get even a part-time job, so they'd be completely dependent on our estate for their upbringing and education."

Many stepmothers want their wills to reflect the needs of the beneficiaries, favoring younger or more dependent children. However, because their ideas of need often differ from their husbands', these women hesitate to write wills that simply leave their assets to their husbands' discretion. They worry that, after their deaths, their husbands will decide to distribute assets differently than they had intended. They want to be sure that, if they die first or if the couple dies together, their wills will protect their own, younger children's interests by limiting the amount their older stepchildren will receive.

Mia Jordan, whose stepchildren refuse even to *visit* when she is home, strongly opposes any will that treats her stepchildren equally. "The truth is," she admits, "that I don't think Bob's kids deserve a penny from us, after the way they've treated us. They've been horrible to Bob, our children *and* me. I want some kind of written guarantee that, if I die first, Bob won't try to resolve the problems with his kids through the distribution of our assets. As long as our will can't prevent that, I can't be content with it. It's not that I want to punish them by not leaving them our money. It's that I see no reason to reward them for what they've done. And certainly not with assets that would otherwise pass to my kids."

Women like Mia feel that, even *after* death, they will need to be vigilant, protecting their children's interests from their stepchildren. Knowing that their stepchildren can easily influence their husbands, they cynically expect the worst and refuse to sign any will that might jeopardize the future welfare of their children. Ironically, *without* wills, they fail to protect their children's interests at all.

These stepmothers often find that their attitudes toward their wills are colored by other issues. They say that they cannot deal separately with issues of visitation, custody, finances, wills and support because they do not *experience* them separately. The issues are seen as overlapping and frustrating aspects of stepmothering.

For stepmothers like Mia, visitation is the biggest problem influencing their views on wills. "Trying to enforce Bob's visitation rights through the courts has been an ordeal for us," she says. "My adrenaline pumps out of control for days before each hearing. I worry about how stressed or hurt Bob will get. I get angry with Bob's ex-wife and kids for putting us through all this. I get frustrated because, although I'm tremendously *involved* in their legal fights, I'm not a *party* to them. I'm forced to sit on the sidelines, wrestling with anxiety, conflict and legal fees."

Ongoing legal battles over stepchildren's visits can be particularly difficult because, even though stepmothers' lives are directly affected by the *outcome*, they are not considered part of the legal *process*. Further, after they endure the stress and the cost, they discover that a court order of visitation is difficult to enforce. If the parent with primary physical custody refuses to cooperate with the decisions, the other parent may face ever-escalating efforts, including obtaining court orders to force the children to visit, having the other parent cited for contempt and, ultimately, trying to obtain physical custody of the children by proving that the custodial parent has deliberately alienated the children.

"What would the point of *that* be, though?" Mia asks. "Why would we want *custody* of two kids who've been taught to despise us? Besides, Bob doesn't want to put his kids through any more fights. I agree. We've given up on visitation. But, when it comes to our wills, it's a different story. I can't suddenly forget what's been said at the visitations hearings or how difficult Bob's kids have made our lives. I can't lovingly treat my stepchildren the same as my own, just because it's time to write my will. In fact, even though they won't speak to me now, someday they'll know exactly how I feel, when they read my will."

Some stepmothers explain that their wills are the only way they can effectively express themselves to their stepchildren. Like Mia, they are powerless in the face of the financial and legal battles that have resulted from their husbands' former marriages. Many feel unprotected from the outcomes of these battles and frustrated by the limits of their own legal options.

"I may sound harsh," says Joyce, another rejected stepmother. "They *are* still only teenagers and they *were* the victims of divorce. Nevertheless, I'm convinced that, at some point, they have to begin to rise above all that. My husband and I can't change the past. We can't even change their attitudes or behavior. But we don't have to tolerate everything, either. If it comes down to the dollars in our wills, the one thing we *can* limit, then I think that's the way to tell them that they've gone too far."

Some stepmothers do not want to include their stepchildren in their wills because they resent the amounts of money their husbands have already paid in child support. Others, whose stepchildren are so alienated that they won't even speak to them, sometimes harbor resentments that their husbands must pay child support at all. A few don't complain about supporting alienated stepchildren until they are eighteen, but resent funding anything beyond that.

"Nick will be ready for college in three years," Mia declares. "Amy will begin when he graduates. Their mother writes Bob hostile notes, demanding to know what he 'intends to do' about their college educations. The law where we live says that children who alienate themselves from their parents are not entitled to *any* support after they turn eighteen. But Bob says he doesn't want his children to have to go to community college, when there's money to pay for almost any school where they'd be accepted. Again, there's a discrepancy between what *Bob* feels and what *I* feel. Even if there are funds to send them to whatever college they want, I'm still opposed to contributing a dime that the law doesn't require, until they decide to treat me and my children with kindness and respect. If they're part of our family enough to get tuition, they should be part of it enough to visit, communicate and be responsible to the other members of the family."

These women are enmeshed in a legal and financial tangle that they barely understand. Even when they try to sort issues out rationally, they find that their emotions color their perceptions and that they have difficulty deciding what is, objectively, fair. Unable to agree with their husbands, besieged by lawsuits involving their husbands' ex-wives, rejected by their stepchildren, they suffer from a sense of powerlessness and frustration that is often expressed openly for the first time when they write their wills.

Financial Chains

Some men did not do well financially in their divorces. Many felt so guilty about leaving that they tried to compensate by giving virtually *all* their marital property to their wives. Others wanted to get out of their marriages so badly that they "bought" their divorces by handing their ex-wives large settlements. When they married these men, many stepmothers realized that their financial lives would forever be in turmoil because of their husbands' preexisting agreements with their former wives.

Others, however, discovered this only later. Although court orders dividing a divorcing couple's property are "carved in stone" and final, such is *not* the case with child support orders. Support orders can be modified any time one of the parents can show the court that there has been a change of circumstances. Although the paying parent *can* have the amount reduced, it is generally the receiving parent who seeks an increase when the payer's circumstances improve.

When Maggie Joyner married Brad, a business consultant, four years ago, she expected their financial road to be rocky. "Brad simply gave his ex-wife, Maria, everything. Maria got all their savings, the house, the car, the investments. She also got Brad to agree to pay for all 'unusual expenses' that would later arise for their son, Josh.

"For most kids, 'unusual expenses' may not mean much. Maybe braces or boy scout camp. But for Josh, 'unusual expenses' far outnumber the 'usual' ones. Oh, we pay for braces and camp, karate and music lessons. But mostly, we pay for drug rehabilitation and therapists."

It is difficult for stepmothers like Maggie to accumulate savings or even plan their expenses because their stepchildren are forever incurring significant, often unplanned, costs. Some, whose husbands agreed to pay *all* such costs, find that their family budgets are completely destroyed when these costs occur. Even those whose husbands have not agreed to cover *all* such costs, find that unexpected bills, whether for dental work or drama lessons, can precipitate bitter disputes about who's to pay. And, even when the parents eventually agree to share the costs, those disputes often deplete everyone's emotions and energy and establish new resentments.

Stepmothers who do not initially realize the extent of their husbands' financial obligations to their stepchildren often are stunned when they find out later. Even though they agree that their husbands should share financial responsibility for their stepchildren, they are convinced that there should be *some* reasonable limits to that responsibility.

Like Mia, Molly, Maggie and many others, they are irritated that their husbands' ex-wives, through the stepchildren, seem to have permanent access to their families' savings. One stepmother complains, "My husband's ex-wife, Liz, has already sued three times for increases in support, even though Stu has always paid fully and on time. She sued us when Stu opened his own office. She sued us after our second child was born. She sued us when we bought our house. It seems that, whenever we have something to be happy about, or whenever we take a step toward realizing *our* goals, she steps in to take some of it away."

Another concludes, "What bothers me most about our legal situation is that our possessions, savings and property will always be subject to examination and attachment by my husband's former family. What's ours is not private. What's ours is not necessarily even *ours*. And even if the courts say they *can't* have it, they can still demand to know *what* we have, what we've earned, what I've earned, what we've put aside for our kids. Our finances are an open book. We can't separate my husband's ex-wife and kids from our personal assets, even though they've long since separated us from their hearts."

Having learned how critical money matters can be, some stepmothers are determined that they and their husbands take special care planning and writing their wills. Even some couples who are currently childless discuss their wills as part of their family planning process.

Maggie and Brad are hoping to have a baby sometime next year. "I wanted the 'will thing' to be decided now," Maggie says, "so it will be clear, precise and uncontestable, not a source of rivalry or anger between Josh and some little half sister or half brother."

In writing their wills, Brad and Maggie considered the ages and parentage of their beneficiaries, and took note of Josh's tendency to addiction. "My earnings, or whatever I can save from them," Maggie declares, "would go to *our* child. Brad's assets would be divided evenly between *his* children, but they'd be doled out differently. The younger child, as a dependent minor, would get more cash up front. Josh, because of his drug history, would receive checks in small amounts over a long period of time."

Stepmothers like Maggie find that *any* positive financial action they can take, even in the realm of the long-range or hypothetical, is helpful. Their wills sometimes provide opportunities for them to assert their own wishes and exert some control. "Our plans for our wills are premature, in a way, since our baby hasn't even been conceived yet," Maggie smiles. "But it's been fun to imagine our baby as a real, legitimate person, instead of as a mere possibility. Besides, planning my will helps take my mind off worrying about how we'll pay for my stepson's next 'unusual expense.'"

Balancing Act

Stepmothers of disturbed or troubled stepchildren often have special problems concerning custody, visitation or finances. Many feel like referees at boxing matches whenever legal or material issues arise concerning their stepchildren.

Jill Sterling's stepson, Charlie, attempted suicide when faced with the prospect of changing custody to live with his father. The uncertainty of where "home" is, the competition between parents and Charlie's own pressures to please his father all contributed to his internal conflicts.

"I see *everybody's* point of view," Jill laments. "But I don't know who's right or wrong, much less how to please everyone or fix anything.

"My husband, Michael, thinks boys should live with their fathers during their teenage years. Pure, sincere belief. Michael doesn't see Charlie as he *is*. He sees him as he *wishes* him to be. Ironically, this is largely because Charlie *doesn't* live with us and Michael's illusions aren't shattered on a daily basis. The fact is that Michael gives Charlie choices that he's too immature to make. Asking Charlie to choose where he wanted to live was *much* more than he could handle.

"Ellen, Michael's ex, wants *all* of Charlie's plans made by and through her. She wants to relieve Charlie of *all* responsibility for his life. Ever since the suicide attempt, I tend to agree with her, but Michael says we are being overprotective and that Charlie will never learn to cope with reality if he's not given increasing doses of responsibility.

"And me, I'm caught in the middle, trying to make peace. But, more than anything, I want to have a little bit of space to raise my *own* children."

Many women who have troubled stepchildren find themselves, like Jill, caught between wanting to help and wanting to separate from the trouble. They feel guilty when they try to distance themselves, drained and resentful when they don't.

"I don't argue with Michael about custody," Jill remarks. "But I certainly don't relish the thought of having my stepson live with us. We have two small children of our own who need my attention, and I don't want to take on Charlie's heavy problems full-time. I don't want to have to monitor Charlie's every move and word for signs of imminent self-destruction. It's exhausting, depressing and frustrating. I really want time out, time just to focus on my own kids."

Custody is not the only legal issue of concern to stepmothers like Jill. Many worry that their husbands' conflicts, anxieties and guilts lead them to favor their troubled stepchildren over their own children financially. This tendency particularly concerns them when they consider writing their wills.

Jill explains, "Michael aches for Charlie so badly that I think he tends to overlook our two kids. Take our wills, for example. We have *major* arguments about our wills. Michael wants us to leave a third of our estate to Charlie. I refuse. I want to leave *my* fifty percent to *our* children, Beth and Billy, and I think *his* fifty percent should be divided equally among *his* three children. That would give Beth and Billy most of our estate, but Charlie will also inherit from his mother. Beth and Billy won't."

Many stepmothers want their wills to be based on similar formulas, in which parentage is balanced against other possible sources of inheritance. Some look for alternative ways to protect what they see as their children's share of their estate. For Jill, the dispute about percentages in the wills continues, but war has been declared in other areas. "Michael took out a five-hundred-thousand-dollar life insurance policy and named Charlie as beneficiary. I was furious! What about *our* children?

"I responded by taking out a one-million-dollar policy on Michael's life, and naming Billy and Beth beneficiaries. Michael exploded. He just didn't see that if something were to happen to him, I'd be stuck with a modest salary, a huge mortgage and two small children to raise and educate. His *only* thoughts were that he wanted to leave poor, sensitive Charlie well-off. When I explained *my* policy to him, I had to be real basic. It was like hitting him with a two-by-four even to get him to *listen* to me."

Many couples eventually agree to compromises that please neither of them. They set up trust funds or designate other divisions of their assets, but their compromises rarely seem "fair" to either of them. Often, although they compromise, the real issues are not resolved; there remains an underlying skepticism about each spouse's intention to adhere to agreed terms.

"I'm not sure I trust Michael where Charlie's concerned," Jill admits. "He's too identified and involved to be fair-minded. I know that if I die Michael will look after our kids, but I really don't know how well, compared to how he'll look after Charlie."

Jill and women like her are hurt by their own distrust, but, over time, most accept their husbands' attitudes. Instead of trying to change them, they employ "defensive" estate planning, creating independent estates for their own children.

Stepmothers who remain without wills and rely on their husbands to divide their estates often remain worried about their own children's futures, angry with their spouses and resentful of their stepchildren. By contrast, those who plan their estates independently feel at ease, in control and at peace about their stepchildren's problems, their husbands' conflicts and their own children's security.

Hear No Evil

Some women whose stepchildren are grown say that issues regarding money, visitation and wills still cause so much tension in their marriages that they avoid the topics altogether. They rarely discuss these subjects with their husbands because they want to avoid arguments. Although most of these couples have wills, the wives often have no idea what is written in their husbands' and say that their husbands are only generally aware of what's in theirs.

"I don't want to know," Jessie Solomon says. She married Mark, a psychiatrist, two years ago. "I've left my entire estate to our son, Adam. Mark must know that, and I'd imagine he must have provided for his older children in his. I'm sure he wouldn't expect me to take care of them if he dies first."

Like Jessie, many stepmothers who marry after they have established successful careers and acquired substantial assets on their own prefer to write their wills independently and to keep their savings separate from their husbands'. Those whose husbands are also financially secure often use their own wills to secure the futures of their children, expecting that their husbands will decide independently how to divide their own estates.

For many of these women, money is a manageable issue, as long as it remains separate from their marriages. For others, money reflects other, deeper divisions within their relationships.

"I'm with Mark," Jessie explains, "because I can't be without Mark. I adore my husband. I really don't care about his money. I have my own. If Mark dies tomorrow and leaves everything to my stepchildren, our son and I wouldn't notice it financially. But if he leaves it all to me, I wouldn't want the responsibility of dividing his property among me and his children. I'm *sure* he knows that, because I've refused to be involved either with his will *or* my stepchildren. He *must* know I don't want to deal with them. The truth is I don't *care* what he gives them. I don't want to know about it."

Security Guard

Many other stepmothers with adult stepchildren believe that they must be forever vigilant about setting limits concerning visits and financial matters because, despite their ages, their stepchildren will use any opportunity to take advantage of their fathers.

"During the first six years of our marriage," Marla Jenson recalls, "I watched Steve shell out a *fortune*. Steve's always paid more than what his support agreement called for. Sometimes he's just given them money. Sometimes they've sued to get it. But it is my opinion that money has always been the rope that his former family has used to hang on to Steve."

Some stepmothers say that their husbands feel responsible for paying for their adult stepchildren's expenses because they are trying to assuage their guilt about their divorces through money. Others see their husbands as completing "unfinished business" by funding their adult children's education or financing their careers or other expenses.

Although many of these stepmothers understand their husbands' motivations, some find that their feelings have changed as a result of their husbands' extravagant indulgence of their stepchildren.

"Steve knows that I know that he's paying more than he has to," Marla says, "but he does it to show them that he loves them. I don't think he realized, until recently, how his habit of throwing money at them affected my image of him or my feelings for him. He looked weak to me. Spineless. When I confronted him about the money, early in our marriage, he told me, 'My hands are tied. It's in the agreement.' I knew, though, that there was no way the agreement required him to buy the kids cars when they turned sixteen, or to send Tiffany to Europe with her friends when she graduated high school. I knew he lied to me, and so I saw him not only as weak, but also as dishonest."

Concerned about their perceptions of their husbands and, therefore, their marriages, women like Marla examine their options. Some, realizing that they cannot afford the emotional consequences of perpetually watching over their husbands and guarding their marital resources, decide to take action. Many simply separate and protect a portion of their property.

"I suppose I've become purposefully selfish," says Marla, "to protect my interests from the grabby fingers of Tiffany and the perpetual crises of Eric. I keep my finances independent of Steve's, as much as I can. I have separate investments, savings and checking arrangements. My will leaves something to Steve, but almost everything goes to our daughter, Sara. His will leaves most everything to me. And, be assured, *my* name appears on *all* of Steve's property and accounts."

Marla's "selfish" policy works for her only superficially; it doesn't help her husband deal with his guilt, prevent him from overindulging his children or enhance her romantic image of him. However, Marla realizes that for the sake of her marriage she must do what she can to reduce her sense of helplessness and financial loss. "I keep our books. I insist on it. I need to feel some control over the money."

Disagreements about their adult stepchildren's expenses are so difficult for some stepmothers that they actually put their marriages on the line. Marla admits, "I've considered telling Steve that if he sends Tiffany on one more vacation, or rents her one more apartment, or pays for one more semester of courses that Eric doesn't complete, I'll leave. But I can't bear the thought of really leaving, or of tearing Sara away from her dad, or of breaking up with him over his children. So, instead of leaving, I've chosen to balance the output of money by giving Sara and myself equal or greater amounts than what Steve gives Eric and Tiffany. As his bank balance diminishes, Steve is realizing that he simply *must* limit what he gives them.

"But what I *wish*," Marla declares, "is that I could have some kind of legal agreement that would put a lid on the amount Steve spends on Tiffany and Eric. The same kind of agreement his ex-wife had that guaranteed her a certain amount, only the counterpart to that agreement. I'd want it to limit the amount, so it won't end with Tiffany and Eric basking and relaxing on a luxury yacht, while we scramble for small change to get on a bus."

Under One Umbrella

Stepmothers with physical custody of their stepchildren often experience unique visitation and financial issues. Many feel that every time their families reach equilibrium, their stepchildren's mothers visit and throw everyone off balance again. Because their stepchildren often have difficulty maintaining simultaneous close relationships with both mothers and stepmothers, the most difficult issues for these women usually concern the emotional adjustments surrounding parental visits.

One stepmother explains, "When my stepdaughter visits her mother, she lives by different rules. She can stay up late, go to bed without a bath, watch as much television as she wants. There are no clear rules. When she comes back here, she thinks I have nerve asking her to clean up her room or brush her hair."

Most of these stepmothers find that the emotional effects of parental visits are visible primarily in their stepchildren's behavior. They dread these visits because they feel helpless to prevent the aftermath. Some try to discuss the problems with their stepchildren, explaining that it *is* difficult to move from parent to parent and home to home, but that each home is different, and that, in each, they must follow the appropriate routines. But these discussions, at best, touch only the surface.

"My stepson misses his mother," one stepmother claims. "They can't get along. They argue all the time. But, even though our home is more peaceful for him, he misses her when he's here. He always returns from his mom's agitated, with some emotion unexpressed or something left unfinished."

Visitation is not the only legal issue that affects stepmothers with primary physical custody differently than others. Some receive child support payments from their stepchildren's mothers. Others find that, in the event that their husbands predecease them, they have unique concerns regarding wills and subsequent custody rights.

Many of those who have wills in which they and their husbands simply sign everything over to the other consider their husband's wills to be tremendous acts of faith. Julie Sinclair was thirty-one when she married Trevor, then thirty-seven. An attorney, Trevor advised that they write their wills right away. "At that time, I had no children," Julie comments. "Trevor had three. If he dies first, I'm completely in charge of his estate. The money is to go to me and I'm to have absolute authority to determine what to do with it."

For custodial stepmothers, control of finances is essential to raising their stepchildren. But, upon their husbands' deaths, many might lose physical custody of their stepchildren. "Trevor and I have discussed all the possible scenarios," Julie says. "He dies and the children choose to live with me. He dies and the children choose to live with their mother. The children choose to live with their mother and she chooses to exploit the estate to upgrade her own lifestyle at their expense, and so on. Trevor has advised me of his wishes in each case, and his will gives me total control. It's really a tremendous responsibility."

Like Jill, Maxine and many others, stepmothers with physical custody often discover that having a child of their own forces them to reexamine their wills. But most find that, unlike Maxine's, their husbands have no problems with inequities among their children's financial resources. The fathers are, in fact, often more concerned with how these inequities might affect the relationships of the half siblings than they are with the inequities themselves.

"My parents have set up a trust for our daughter, Emily," Julie says. "My will leaves my medical practice and a few other assets to her. Emily will probably have a lot more money than the other three kids. Trevor and I have talked about how this may influence their relationships. It's our hope that, by the time Emily gets her money, the others, who are much older, will be well-established and successful in whatever careers they choose, so it won't matter to them *what* Emily has."

Overall, stepmothers with physical custody find that simplest is best when it comes to finances. Many share all of their personal accounts and property with their husbands. Property is often held in both names. Some say that this kind of joint ownership not only minimizes the importance of wills, but also makes a statement about the degree of trust and confidence they share with their husbands.

Even among couples who trust each other and share their property, however, problems *can* arise when limited resources must be divided among the children's competing needs. Julie says that this was her experience when Emily approached school age. "Emily will begin first grade the same year Zach begins college. I want Emily to attend a private school. With Zach entering college, Kevin following the next year and Tori starting two years later, I want to be sure that there will be enough money for Emily to have the kind of education I'd like. So, I've opened a separate account for her education. I deposit a certain sum every month, and by the time Emily begins first grade, there should be enough to pay her tuition. I'll continue to feed that account as long as she continues in private school, or as long as I feel it's important to keep money aside for my daughter."

Many custodial stepmothers contribute generously to the costs of raising their stepchildren and see the family's money as a fund to benefit *all* family members. Often, their *only* concern about finances is that their own children might be denied something important because the family's funds are going to their stepchildren. Like Julie, some open separate accounts for their children to insure that such situations will never arise. Although they care about their stepchildren and assist their husbands' efforts to support them, they don't want to deprive their *own* children in the process.

Others see their financial responsibilities for their own children as completely separate from their stepchildren, believing that their stepchildren's finances are, simply, the responsibilities of their parents. They are willing to make necessary sacrifices for the children, but admit that it's far more difficult to sacrifice for children who are not their own.

"The main problem we have with finances is that there never seems to be enough, or at least any extra, money," Julie sighs. "For instance, we desperately needed to get the inside of our house painted, and that would cost several thousand dollars. If we *had* several thousand extra, though, we'd have more important uses for it than painting our house. Maybe we'd fix up the basement and turn it into a family room. Or, maybe Trevor and I could go away alone together for a week or two. I guess that sounds selfish. But it would be nice, once in a while, to spend our money on something besides the kids. Something just for us ... someday ... "

Musical Houses

Just as financial agreements concerning stepchildren are subject to revision, so are custody arrangements. Stepmothers who begin their marriages fully expecting alternating weekend visits by their stepchildren are sometimes surprised when circumstances change and their stepchildren visit more often or even move in permanently.

"I don't want David to live with us, but Alex wants physical custody," declares Jennifer Slade. "I've told Alex that David is with us so much that I don't see the point in getting physical custody. I really don't see what the difference would be in terms of time spent with David. But Alex has a 'Here's the Difference' speech. It has to do partly with support payments being reduced, but mostly it's about the feeling of 'home' or 'belonging' with somebody. Alex wants David to feel he belongs with us, or, rather, with *him*."

Jennifer, however, does not share this goal. Like many other women, she wants her stepson to feel that *her* home is not quite *his*. "Custody is the first issue I've taken a stand on," she says. "I do not want David to live with us. I realize that, in terms of time spent with David, it probably wouldn't be any different. But there's a big difference to me. When David's in my home now, I treat him like a guest. It's a relationship with a distance, a distance I purposely put there. I'll cook

David's favorite dinner, I'll make his bed for him, but I couldn't live with the constant pressure of the servile role I take when he's in my own home."

For many stepmothers, physical custody does not affect how *much* time they spend with their stepchildren; it affects how they *feel* about that time. Although Jennifer's attitudes may not be typical, other stepmothers often find that there is a great psychological difference between a stepchild "visiting" half the time and the stepchild "living with them" half the time. For some, the issues are mostly freedom and territory; for others, like Jennifer, it's a matter of how they define their place in their marriages.

"When Alex and I married," Jennifer explains, "we didn't have physical custody of David. Getting that custody now would mean that the 'deal' we made when we took our vows would be changed, and that just isn't right. I know that there are no guarantees in life, and that we said 'for better or worse,' but I'd like to try for 'better' rather than inviting 'worse.'"

Some stepmothers feel left out of the decisions about physical custody, as if the parents and the stepchildren have more to say about the decisions than they do. This sense of powerlessness is a repetitive theme among many of the stepmothers we interviewed. Like Jennifer, they discuss their problems with clarity and detail, but have no idea how to solve them.

"David is fifteen years old. At his age, the court would probably allow David to choose where he wants to live. Either choice would cause problems. Let's say David decides he *doesn't* want to live with us. Alex could never handle that. My fear is that he couldn't stand to see himself as the loser in the battle, so he'd blame David's decision on me. It would be, 'You made David feel unwelcome; he knows you don't love him' and on and on. I'd be the ultimate loser.

"If David *does* choose us, or if I give in and say, 'Fine, David can live here,' what's *that* going to be like for me? I'd be miserable and our marriage would be strained, but it's strained anyway, because I've said I don't want David living here. Whatever happens with custody, there's the domino effect. One problem inviting another and another indefinitely."

Physical custody of their stepchildren is often of particular relevance to stepmothers whose husbands don't want to have children with them. "When Alex said he didn't want another child, I struggled,"

Jennifer sighs. "I was heartbroken. But I tried to focus on the bright side. Without children, I, and we, could be spontaneous. Alex and I could be free to do what we wanted, without the responsibilities that parents have. We could pack our bags any time and fly off somewhere. We could indulge ourselves, spend time and attention on each other instead of on kids.

"But I was forgetting about David. We spend a huge amount of time and money each week on David. As it is, we have the freedom but we don't have the time. And if we get custody, if David *lives* with us, we won't even have the freedom."

Some disappointed, childless stepmothers hope, as Jennifer did, that their husbands will become more available to them as their stepchildren get older. Many find out otherwise.

"The latest shock is that my husband has agreed to pay for David's college education, *without* help from his ex-wife. Alex's need to prove his love to David is never-ending. I wonder what Alex plans for *our* future. Does he ever think of us growing old together, or spending our time and money on each other? Are all his thoughts about David? Where do *I* fit into all of this? The truth is that I'm afraid to find out."

Jennifer believes that her situation is dire. But she agrees with other, less desperate stepmothers, that most attempts to understand financial and custody arrangements *prior* to marriage are futile because *everything* can change. After several years of marriage, many say that they were naive to think that any legal documents were final. Just because parents initially agree to certain terms concerning child support, visitation or custody does not mean that they will be content with those agreements as time goes on and circumstances change. No such agreement, stepmothers find, is permanent.

"The point is," Jennifer states, "I *thought* I knew what I was in for, in terms of finances and visitation anyway. But nothing is certain. It's all up to the parents and the courts. I'm powerless when Alex willingly writes support checks for triple the amount I read about when I got married. I'm powerless when he says he'll pay for David to go to college. I'm powerless when Alex agrees to let David visit us three or four nights each week. And, ultimately, if David and Alex and his ex-wife agree that David should *live* here, I'll be powerless, too. That is, powerless except to say, 'No.' I suppose...but I hate to think about it...that I can always leave."

Legal and Material Communication

The best defense for stepmothers against feelings of powerlessness in regard to legal, material and financial issues is open communication with their husbands. Those who do communicate—although they may not *control*, much less *like*, the outcome of custody and support disputes—feel they are definitely part of the decision-making process. It is their belief that most stepmothering issues, whether about finances, custody, wills or other topics, reflect other fundamental issues within their marriages. The first step in achieving satisfaction as a stepmother is realizing a satisfying marital relationship and an active, influential role as a partner and wife.

Advice From Stepmothers on Legal and Material Issues

1.   **Find out what the existing agreements are.** Discuss, as early in your relationship as possible, what agreements your husband (or financé) has made concerning custody, visitation and financial support for his children. Make sure you understand not only what he's agreed to, but what his *attitude* is toward the agreement, so that you know what he *wants* the agreements to become with time. Talk about your feelings on these issues *before* you marry, if you can, so that neither of you is surprised later by the other's goals or opinions. Be sure you understand and concur on the basic philosophy or goals of these important agreements.

2.   **Realize that any existing agreement may change.** Either parent can petition the courts for changes in custody or support any time that there is a change of circumstances. The original order is not permanent. Be prepared for changes to affect your commitment of time and finances to your stepchildren.

3.   **Know how you want to manage your assets and plan your estate.** Be aware of what assets you and your husband have, whether they are joint or separate. Be aware of the options you have in terms of estate planning. If you have children of your own, be careful to plan for them and for your stepchildren independently, so that you and your husband are each satisfied with the provisions made for each child. If you and your husband are planning to have children, discuss how the birth of a child will affect your estate and how you will adjust your plan to include the new addition.

4.   **Be prepared for the unexpected.** No matter how you plan or how closely you and your husband agree on financial and legal matters, the unanticipated *will* happen. Custody and support are just a few of the items that could be affected by circumstances beyond your control. Be aware, when you accept the role of stepmother, that you're accepting all the variables in the lives of your stepchildren *and* their mother. Plan for the unpredictable. Know what you would do if physical custody changes or support orders increase. Identify issues that would be most difficult for you to deal with and plan, with your husband, how to be prepared for them.

5.   **Consult your own attorney before the wedding.** Learn how your intended spouse's obligations to his children and ex-wife can affect you. Discuss how existing custody and financial agreements might have an impact on your marriage, including property, future children and other factors. Prepare yourself with knowledge of the situation, your rights and your legal options. Do everything you can *before* your marriage to protect yourself from legal and material issues which may arise *during* your marriage.

FIVE

The Ex-Wife

"I've never even met her," says one stepmother, "but I sense her every day like an unseen, sinister presence in my life."

"She's not exactly an *ex*-wife," states another, "she's his *other* wife. At least that's how she behaves."

"She's not *his* ex-wife," claims a third, "she's *our* ex-wife. She's part of our marital package."

Fully half of the stepmothers we interviewed claim that most of the problems they encounter with their stepchildren are the direct result of problems with the children's mothers. Fewer than one in five have positive, or even comfortable, relationships with the mothers of their stepchildren.

The problems between mothers and stepmothers vary, ranging from finances to jealousy about the marriage, to competition and power plays involving the children. The amount of actual contact between mothers and stepmothers also varies. A few stepmothers have intense relationships and frequent direct contact with their stepchildren's mothers; others have never even seen them.

The mothers also maintain a wide range of relationships with their ex-husbands, from affectionate to belligerent. Some have been apart for years; others are relatively recent divorcées. Many are happily divorced, with new, satisfying, successful lives. Some have remarried, and a few have even had additional children with their new husbands. A number of ex-wives, however, are "stuck in the past," and some blame stepmothers for the breakup of their marriages and their own subsequent problems.

Despite the vast differences in post-divorce adjustments, personal compatibility and levels of communication between stepmothers and mothers, one theme emerges consistently: stepmothers are surprised by the amount of *power* held by their stepchildren's mothers. This power is not completely unexpected as it pertains to the stepchildren or even to their fathers. What stuns stepmothers is the impact it has on their *own* lives.

The Faceless Enemy

"I've never met her," says Mia Jordan. "I've never even *seen* her. I've seen pictures of her, but her face has always been so small in them that I can't see her features. If I passed Kate on the street, I wouldn't recognize her. Nor would she, I'm sure, know me. In all the years I've been with Bob, I've spoken to his ex-wife only once, when she screamed obscenities at me on the phone."

Stepmothers like Mia encounter mothers who are so angry that they refuse to have any contact with them at all. Many of these stepmothers find it difficult to understand this anger, much less why it sometimes lingers for years after the divorce. Even when they know the facts surrounding the divorces, they are perplexed to discover that neither the passage of time nor the efforts they make to be "good" stepmothers diminish the hostility of their husbands' ex-wives. Because they cannot discuss parenting issues with their stepchildren's mothers, some find it difficult to take care of their stepchildren. Many feel personally wounded that they are judged and rejected by women who do not even know them. Most of all, they are baffled that their stepchildren's mothers seem oblivious to the harm that their hostility can inflict on others, including their own children.

"Kate is a woman I cannot fathom," Mia Jordan sighs. "She *nourishes* her anger. She doesn't want to let go of it and move on. She's devoted to the task of hurting my husband in any way she can, even after eight years and her own remarriage. Her fury surfaces in incredible ways, too. Like, she never lets the kids use the toys or clothes we send them. We found out from Kate's mother that our gifts go straight to some thrift shop for resale. The children are never allowed to keep them."

Some stepmothers, like Mia, believe that their stepchildren's mothers are still in love with their husbands and that that love, frustrated and rejected, has fermented with time, changing to hatred. Unable to vent their anger on their former husbands, some of these "scorned" ex-wives find new targets in their children's stepmothers, using their children as weapons.

"Kate has filled Nick and Amy's minds with lies about Bob and me. She calls me a 'bitch' and Bob a 'bum.' She told the kids that Bob left her because of an affair with me. The truth is that I didn't even *date* Bob until after they'd separated. Kate invented that scenario, but I'm sure the children believe, since their mother told them it was so, that *I* broke up their otherwise 'happy' family.

"Bob and I have never been able to contradict what Kate says. We've told the kids the truth about how we met and when we began to date, but we could see, by the looks on their faces, that they didn't believe us. Why would they believe a 'bitch' and a 'bum'?"

Many stepmothers are similarly on the defensive with their stepchildren. Their stepchildren dislike them, but they have no idea why, since they are unaware of what their stepchildren's mothers have said about them. They struggle to squelch rumors, expose lies, defuse tempers, but even if they discover what has prejudiced their stepchildren, they find it difficult to defend themselves with credibility, since they are contradicting "what Mommy says."

Many in similar situations are deeply concerned about the effects of the ex-wives' anger on their stepchildren. By turning their children against their fathers, hampering their children's relationships with their stepmothers and blocking communication, these mothers impair the development of their own children.

"Kate's example teaches her children that it's okay *not* to compromise, *not* to communicate and work out problems, *not* to respect their father. Instead, she encourages them to insist that things be *their* way, damaging their ability to conduct successful relationships on their own. Kate is so angry, though, that she doesn't *consider* what she's doing to the children."

These stepmothers mourn the relationships they might have had with their stepchildren, if not for the fury of their stepchildren's mothers. Many also regret, when they have their *own* children, that relationships between half- or stepsiblings fall victim to that anger. They feel sorry for their stepchildren, their husbands and themselves, but almost never express sympathy for the ex-wives.

"My daughter cries when Nick's or Amy's name comes up," Mia says. "She's made Nick into a superhero fantasy character. I hear her playing with her friends, saying, 'My *brother's* going to get those bad guys.' It breaks my heart how badly she misses them. Kate has the power to let go and let us all heal, but she won't."

Stepmothers like Mia, confronted with an anger that they cannot defuse and with a woman who refuses to communicate—let alone *cooperate*—often feel hopeless and frustrated. They encounter emotion that has grown larger than whatever caused it, that has been distorted and refueled by time.

The Ghost of Marriage Past

Although some stepmothers are sorry that they have no relationships with their husbands' ex-wives, others prefer it that way. Although they have no personal gripes against their husbands' former wives, they avoid having any contact with them.

Many of these women have grown stepchildren. Their husbands' divorces have been final for years; child support, property settlements and alimony have all been paid. Most believed, therefore, that the ex-wife was "gone for good," relegated to events and relationships of the distant, fading past.

"I was sure that I was going to have the rest of Mark's life for our son and me," Jessie Solomon says. "But it's funny. You can't control anything. The past doesn't go away. It's part of the present. Mark's ex-wife, Lynne, is being recycled into Mark's life because of their grandson. They share children, and now they share a grandchild. *They*, Mark and *Lynne, not* Mark and me, share the grandchild. *They* are grandparents. People congratulate *them*, not me. *They* get the attention. *They* share the memories of babies who are now having babies of their own. Whenever the family gathers, despite everything that's happened, Mark and Lynne appear as a couple again. My role is unclear. I'm an outsider. I loathe these events. But I go along to protect my turf, so people will see that Mark is *my* husband, not hers."

These stepmothers find it difficult to accept the fact that, because they share children, their husbands and their former wives will remain involved with each other, at some level, throughout their lives. They feel uncomfortable at events that require the presence of both their stepchildren's parents. Like Jessie, however, most realize that such occasions are not easy for the ex-wives, either.

"I don't blame Lynne for any of this awkwardness. She's a lady. We don't make good eye contact, but we *are* cordial. I suspect that she misses Mark, seeing him again after all this time. Maybe that's just my impression. I don't know. But I don't like seeing them together. Who knows what he feels for his ex-wife when he sees her nuzzling their grandchild? I don't want to deal with that question. I want us to be left alone, in peace, without Mark's entire past knocking at our door. My ex-husband doesn't go to dinner with us, but Lynne does when there's a family occasion, and she'll do so more frequently, I imagine, as more grandchildren arrive and more occasions arise. It makes me want to scream."

Although Jessie's feelings are extreme, they reflect those of a number of stepmothers who experience a definite, threatening rivalry with the bonds formed in their husbands' pasts. When events like weddings or births make it clear that these attachments have not been *broken* but merely *changed*, many of these stepmothers find reality hard to accept. Under masks of polite civility, they struggle with jealousy, insecurity and resentment. Even though their marriages are sound, they are unable to overcome or control these feelings and see no indication that they, or their situations, will change.

"Here I am, the evil witch jealously cursing the royal baby. I know that's how I sound, but I'm tired of all these reappearing, never-dying, ghost relationships. Lynne's relationship with Mark supposedly died *years* ago. But here it is, reincarnated. She and her progeny won't go away. They're my demons, here to stay."

The Other Wife

While some stepmothers have difficulty seeing their husbands' former wives at the occasional family reunion, others are besieged by constant contact. These women are convinced that their stepchildren's mothers will *never* let go of their husbands; they believe, in fact, that they still love them and want them back. Their husbands' ex-wives call these women, sometimes several times a day, clinging to *them*, as a means of reaching their husbands.

"Maria isn't Brad's *ex*-wife; she's his *other* wife," explains Maggie Joyner. "She'll call up and suggest that she and Brad buy joint Christmas gifts for their son, Josh, and even for Josh's grandparents. She tries to get Brad involved in all kinds of schemes, even though she's married again. Her new husband tries to discourage her involvement with Brad, but he can't. She was married to Brad for eighteen years and she didn't want the divorce. So, she never lets him forget that they'll be forever bound together because they are the proud parents of Josh. Josh is her ticket to Brad and always will be."

As they become aware that their stepchildren's mothers have no intention of letting go, some stepmothers panic, become threatened and try to minimize contact with their husbands' ex-wives. Most, however, realize that this clutchiness is probably more annoying to their husbands than it is to them, and try to ease the situation in any way they can. But, like Maggie, they often find that there is a limit to their patience, that their efforts go unnoticed and that they make little progress over time.

Some stepmothers find themselves so involved with their husbands' ex-wives and their stepchildren that they become confused about their roles and the boundaries of their families. They include ex-wives in family plans, extending themselves across the lines of divorce. In an effort to protect their husbands from constant contact, they become the liaisons for the stepchildren's mothers. Most find these roles as demanding as they are thankless.

"When Josh graduated from high school, his mother threw a party. She saw to it that toasts were given, poems were written and read aloud. Everything was about 'Mom and Dad,' giving thanks to Josh's 'parents.' There wasn't a word or a mention of all the years I'd spent in my stepson's life or the efforts I'd made to get him to do his homework, go to class without getting stoned or keep him from dropping out of school. No reference to me at all.

"That's just one incident, but it's typical. She leans on me for help with Josh. She talks to me more than she does to Brad about their son. But she never, never gives me recognition as Josh's stepmother. I don't expect it, really. After all, Maria introduces herself, refers to herself in Brad's presence, as 'the first wife.' As in, 'Hello, I'm the *first* wife.'

She uses that phrase as if it's a rank in order of preference, not chronology."

Some stepmothers feel that, because they have intervened on behalf of their husbands, they know more about their husbands' ex-wives than they should. But they believe that it is essential that they maintain a level of formality with the former wives, even when their patience is taxed and their endurance tested.

One stepmother explained the unique need for mutual respect between mother and stepmother thus: "If I were to meet Wendy socially, I'd probably like her. She's attractive, intelligent and friendly. But *my* picture of her is distorted. Because I see her through the eyes of the man who left her, I see her shortcomings and his disappointments above all else. I know their history through *his* eyes, when, really, I have no right to know what passed between them as husband and wife. But, because I *do* know these things, and because Wendy and I *are* in close touch, I make a conscious effort to be respectful of her and to act like I don't know what I know."

Sensitivity for their husbands' ex-wives, however, does not necessarily gain stepmothers reciprocal respect from the ex-wives *or* from other family members. Further, stepmothers who find themselves locked into relationships with their husbands' ex-wives often have trouble limiting the conversations to topics directly related to their stepchildren.

"Maria heard, probably from my in-laws, that Brad and I are planning to have a baby, so she began asking me questions about my fertility. She asks me if we're 'trying' yet. When I inquired why she felt this was her business, she declared with some indignation, 'Well, this is not just *your* baby, you know. It's the brother or sister of my son!' She is, after all, the 'first wife.' "

Like Maggie, many stepmothers feel conflicted because they have been pulled closer to the ex-wives than they want to be and describe their own roles as buffers, advisers and confidants rather than as friends. Nevertheless, many find themselves becoming oddly fond of their stepchildren's mothers, even though they would much prefer to have less frequent contact and fewer mutual concerns.

"I realize that I actually *like* Maria," Maggie confesses. "How else could I put up with her on a daily basis? I just wish she would back out of my marriage and into her own. I wish she didn't worry about my fertile days each month. I wish she didn't consider Brad's plans when she wants to throw parties or give gifts. Still, although she *wants* to be, Maria isn't a danger to me. Brad left her and leaves her again every chance he gets. She can't accept that, so she hangs on to him and gets me as part of the deal. And I get *her*, Brad's 'other,' not quite 'ex-' wife."

Best Friends

"Rhonda is everywhere," Molly Jerome laughs quietly.

Some stepmothers complain that their husbands ex-wives are not content with merely contacting *them* several times a day; the ex-wives also maintain strong ties with their extended families and social circles. They will not let go of the lives they shared with their husbands, even when their marriages have long been over. And even if they remarry, they remain heavily involved with their former friends and in-laws. Like Molly, stepmothers facing this situation accept their stepchildren's mothers as permanent members of the family. Nevertheless, they have difficulty with the mothers' constant interference in their personal and social lives.

"Rhonda calls me all the time to ask about our social activities," Molly complains. "She involves herself with our friends and socializes with Ed's family. Well, they *were* married for sixteen years, so that's somewhat understandable. But, her motives are not really to retain those relationships. What Rhonda's trying to do is to participate vicariously in our lives and, somehow, become part of our marriage. She actually called me the day we came back from our honeymoon! The phone rang and Rhonda said, 'Tell me, how was it?' I was flabbergasted. But I told her, as dreamily as I could, that it was just perfect. She became speechless, but only momentarily."

Many of these stepmothers would not mind this "friendly" contact by their husbands' ex-wives if they did not believe that it merely masked hostility. They find that even when they respond with genuine friendliness their relationships have a deeper, darker side.

"I don't really mind her calls," Molly admits. "What I mind is her hypocrisy. To me, she acts friendly and chatty. But behind my back she's vicious. Mutual friends and Ed's family have told me what she says about me. She says that I just married Ed for his money and that I curry favor with my stepchildren because they'll be rich one day. That tells me that money is all *she* sees in Ed! She can't imagine that I might *love* him!"

Another stepmother said that her husband's ex-wife gossips about her, unaware that their mutual friends report what they hear: "She told Marv's sister-in-law that she was going to dress to kill for a wedding we were all attending, because she wanted to show Marv 'what he was missing!' What does that imply about me, that she thinks I'm a dog biscuit?"

In order to cope with their aggravation, these stepmothers try to keep sight of the reason they are in touch with their husbands' ex-wives: their stepchildren. No matter how exasperated they become, they tolerate the ex-wives for the sake of their stepchildren. However, because their relationships with the mothers are double-edged, this effort can be tough.

Stepmothers like Molly often feel sorry for their husbands' ex-wives, who are unable to let go of the past and their former relationships. Some believe that the ex-wives are still so in love with their ex-husbands that they will play any role that allows them to stay in touch. Others think that the ex-wives identities are actually linked to their prior marriages, and that without the roles and relationships built during those marriages, they don't know who they are or how to live.

"Rhonda seems to feel incomplete without Ed," Molly concludes. "She's lost without him, so she can't let go. It can be embarrassing. Recently, at a party for a friend, she had one drink too many and, when it was time to leave, she slipped her arm through Ed's and loudly announced, 'Honey, it's time to go!' People stared. Ed froze. I was afraid, for just an instant, that he'd follow her out the door! I hustled through the crowd, took his arm from her and said, just as loudly, 'Sorry, Rhonda, you can't have him back.'"

Secure in their marriages, these stepmothers can afford to be charitably tolerant of their husbands' former wives. However, most do not think that they could change their situations even if they wanted to and feel forced to accept the ex-wives as they are.

"Rhonda will always be part of our lives. The children link us. But, even when the kids are grown, Rhonda will find a way to stick around. I don't find her really threatening. But I know she'll never stop trying to interfere. She'll keep on scheming, whispering and spying as long as she breathes."

With their stepchildren in mind, stepmothers like Molly avoid confrontations and minimize tensions, resentments and jealousies with their husbands' ex-wives. They expect that the ex-wives will forever plot and gossip against them. A few believe that the ex-wives truly want their former husbands back, but most think that they simply, if bitterly, resent the happiness and marital success their former husbands have attained. Whatever their motivations, these ex-wives remain firmly within the family circle, keeping a close, critical eye on what goes on there.

Penance and Punishment

Some stepmothers became involved with their husbands while the men were still married to their former wives. A number admit that their relationships actually precipitated their husbands' divorces. Most, however, believe that these divorces would have occurred eventually, anyway, and that their husbands would have neither noticed nor become involved with them had their prior marriages been successful.

Whether or not those beliefs are accurate, many ex-wives blame stepmothers for their divorces. Some of these scapegoated stepmothers say that the ex-wives find it easier to blame "the new wife" than themselves. Others, however, consciously or not, encourage this blame because they feel guilt about the role they played in their husbands' marital breakups.

"I was always a 'good girl,'" declares Jennifer Slade, "until I met Alex. I was the one who got all A's in school, who never stayed out late. I'd never even walked on the grass, because it was against the rules. But then, I met Alex. I was thirty-three and I fell in love.

"Alex was my professor at night school. He was married, and I *knew* he was married, but, in my defense, I can only say that he told me that he and his wife, Gloria, had been estranged for years and that neither of them cared about the marriage anymore. I was infatuated, in love for the first time, head over heels and, even if Alex had told me Gloria was *mad* for him, I'd have had difficulty staying away. But he didn't tell me that Gloria was mad for him. He told me they were finished, and I believed him. I was naive. I blame myself for that."

Like Jennifer, most stepmothers who harbor guilt about their husbands' divorces are defensive about their pasts, as if they need to exonerate themselves or receive forgiveness. Some of their husbands' ex-wives discovered their affairs and actively, often frantically, tried to win their husbands back. Some stepmothers are haunted by memories of these desperate, jealous wives who struggled to save their doomed marriages.

One stepmother remembers her courtship days with embarrassment and sorrow. "Larry's wife, Paula, went crazy. She became obsessed with me, with what she imagined Larry and I were doing. She actually spied on us. We came home from a movie one night and, while Larry unlocked my door, I saw Paula on her knees, crouching behind the garbage cans next to my building, watching us. Smoking cigarettes and watching us. I didn't know *what* to do. I was so stunned that I just pretended she wasn't there."

Many of these stepmothers feel that they themselves are at fault for humiliating their husbands' former wives. Their sense of culpability taints their roles as wives and stepmothers and impedes their relationships with their stepchildren. Some become passive, accepting or even *inviting* punishment and blame, confused about the basics of "right" and "wrong" in their love relationships.

"When I was dating Alex," Jennifer recalls, "Gloria called me all the time. She used to ask *me* what she could do to hold onto her husband. She grilled me to find out what *I* had that *she* didn't. It was very odd, but I would *talk* to her. Sometimes I even gave her *advice* because she was so frantic! She used to plead with me to give him up, and I knew I should, but I couldn't.

"Finally, Alex moved in with me. He said that, even if I wouldn't marry him, he wouldn't go back to Gloria. His marriage was finished, either way. Again, Gloria called me several times a day, asking if I was happy that I'd destroyed a family and ruined her son's life. I wanted to explain to her that I had *not* been the cause of their breakup, that Alex had decided to leave her *anyway*. But that sounded so cruel that I listened to her, out of guilt."

At the very outset of their roles as stepmothers, these women feel apologetic toward their husbands' ex-wives. That attitude often carries over into their marriages and their relationships with their stepchildren, and it damages their images of themselves.

"I began to think of myself, as I look back, as a husband-stealer. I began to think that it *was* my fault that Gloria's marriage failed. To this day, I still have a shaky self-concept. And I still feel ashamed of the way our marriage began."

Stepmothers like Jennifer and ex-wives like Gloria do not have clear ideas of their own responsibilities or faults. Neither do they assign responsibility or fault to the men who definitely share at least some of both. These women become so engrossed in competing, blaming, defending and apologizing that they forget that the men involved are independent adults who made their own deliberate decisions about their relationships. In feeling guilty about their husbands' divorces, these stepmothers forget that the divorces were, in fact, their *husbands'*, that the *marriages* were their husbands', and that the primary responsibility for *maintaining* those marriages was also their husbands'. Caught up in no-win contests with each other, these wives and ex-wives frequently deny or overlook their husbands' roles.

Stepmothers like Jennifer suffer because they become too identified with their husbands' ex-wives and too involved in the failures of the former marriages. They find it difficult to take charge of their own feelings and forgive themselves for their mistakes. Instead, they leave the power of forgiveness to their husbands' former wives, who are determined to blame and punish them. In fact, most of these stepmothers are so focused on gaining the approval of their husbands, stepchildren and stepchildren's mothers that it does not occur to them that they have the power to take control of their own emotional lives.

Mid-life, Ex-wife Crises

Many stepmothers depict the mothers of their stepchildren as highly unstable, undependable or troubled. While some say that the mothers have *always* had shaky personalities, others attribute their problems to traumas such as divorce. Many ex-wives had particularly difficult adjustments to divorces that they did *not want, and* were forced to enter the singles' scene during middle age. As new divorcées, some panicked, saw their divorces as abandonment and felt suddenly old and jealous, not only of their husbands' new wives, but also of their own youthful children.

Marla Jenson remembers, "My husband's ex, Pam, was extremely angry about the divorce and Steve's remarriage to me. But, when she found out I was pregnant, she went completely nuts. For years she'd hung on to Steve by being the 'mother' of his children, and now I was taking that exclusive title away from her. She herself was now too old to have more children, so she had a real identity crisis. She began dating her daughter Tiffany's male friends. Boys twenty or more years younger than she was. Then she'd tell Tiffany about her relationships, as if she were Tiffany's girlfriend instead of her mother. Pam dressed like a teenager, painted herself with makeup, colored her hair bright red and fixed it in ridiculous, trendy styles. It was embarrassing."

Stepmothers like Marla often express sympathy for the plight of their husbands' ex-wives, but, just as often, they express contempt. They find it difficult to empathize with women who compete with their own children for romantic attachments or who humiliate themselves through openly desperate behavior. Some stepmothers think the ex-wives are trying to hurt their former husbands, exacting revenge by chasing after younger men. Others suspect that they hope their ex-husbands will come to their rescue, reclaiming them and saving them from the perils of "single life." Whatever their motives, according to stepmothers, many former wives find it impossible to leave their ex-husbands alone during this stormy period of adjustment.

"Pam would call our house at all hours of the night, for no apparent reason," Marla recalls. "She'd ask to talk to Steve, but then she'd have nothing to say. Steve was furious about Pam's behavior, but he felt he could do nothing. He thought that if Pam knew she was upsetting him by having affairs with Tiffany's boyfriends, she'd actually be encouraged to have more of these affairs. He thought she wanted to get back at him. So, we tried to ignore Pam's behavior and told Tiffany to grin and bear it, not to be angry, because her mom was just going through 'a tough time.' But *we* saw Pam's affairs with Tiffany's friends as pathetic, futile attempts at revenge."

Even when the dust settles after their divorces, some ex-wives remain unstable. Some stepmothers suspect that the ex-wives have long struggled with emotional problems and that their divorces, as monumental personal catastrophes, finally trigger their defeats. After time passes and these ex-wives either remarry or become accustomed to being single, their problems quietly persist.

Even after stepchildren are grown and ex-wives have rebuilt their lives, these stepmothers find it difficult to trust the resulting calm. Although they are polite and civil to their husbands' former wives, they keep their guard up. Even when they have no evidence that the ex-wives are still unstable, many admit that they cannot recover from the stresses of the past enough to develop open, nondefensive relationships with their husbands' former wives.

"Things *are* calmer for us now," Marla sighs. "Pam seems happily married, and the kids aren't living with her now that they're grown, so we have less contact with her. But we still tread lightly around her. Maybe it's just out of habit. But we have plenty of history with her, and we are not complete fools."

The Mother of Neglect

While stepmothers like Marla are concerned that their husbands' ex-wives are unstable, others worry that they are downright destructive. They describe ex-wives who cannot hold on to jobs, residences or enduring romantic relationships. Some, according to stepmothers, hurt anyone who comes close to them, including their own children.

Maxine James says that Irene, her husband's ex-wife, has been neglectful of her stepdaughter, Tina, to the point of negligence.

"When Gordon and I married, Tina was seven years old. She carried a pacifier with her everywhere we went. I suggested that she leave it in the bedroom and use it only for sleeping. She refused, and her mother insisted that Tina be allowed to have her pacifier any time she wanted it. She sucked on that pacifier until she was nine years old. I was patient for a long time, because I understood that the pacifier offered Tina some security. But she brought it with her to restaurants and malls and while visiting friends. It was damaging her because people thought there was something *wrong* with her."

Although the pacifier was not *dangerous* to Tina per se, Maxine saw it as hurtful, even destructive, to tolerate its use. When women in similar situations see their stepchildren harmed by damaging behaviors, many wish they were therapists rather than stepmothers, so they could effectively counter the negative influences of their stepchildren's mothers.

"Eventually, *I* told Tina that the pacifier would *not* leave the house. She looked at me in surprise and said, 'Okay.' That was all it took. My point here is that no one had set *limits* for Tina before. Her mother had *encouraged* Tina to remain a baby."

Many of these stepmothers try to overlook the behavior of their stepchildren's mothers, but when harmful patterns continue over time, they are often forced to assert themselves on behalf of their stepchildren.

"I was afraid to think that things could really be as bad as they seemed," Maxine admits. "The clues were mostly minor, but there were so many of them that I eventually admitted that Irene might be as pathetic as I feared.

"Tina was always a mess when she arrived at our house. Her hair was dirty and uncombed. She had no table manners, ate with her fingers, rarely used a napkin. Her mother gave her no lessons about taking care of herself, let alone how to behave around others. I had to teach her.

"Besides that, Tina's mother forgets about her. She forgets what time she's supposed to pick her up from our house. Or, she promises to take Tina some place special, like to a movie, and then forgets. Tina is always getting disappointed by her mother."

When they cannot "fix" things for their stepchildren, some stepmothers become frustrated. Unable to get through to either their stepchildren *or* the mothers, some lash out in irrational frustration at their *husbands*, blaming them for the situation.

"I'm angry with Betty for neglecting her daughter," says one stepmother whose ten-year-old stepdaughter is frequently left alone by her mother all night. "But I certainly blame Howard for allowing that neglect. I think he should have done something to put an end to it long ago."

Among the areas most troubling to stepmothers like Maxine is the way their husbands' ex-wives display their private lives in front of their children. Some say the ex-wives have been unable to sustain long-term relationships with men and have paraded a steady stream of male companions past the children. They worry both that their stepchildren are confused by these relationships and that they are being provided with negative lessons about love.

"Irene gets involved in dead-end affairs with married men and tells Tina about them. One week Tina will be full of sunshine and cheer, announcing that her mother has a new boyfriend. The next week, very depressed, Tina will tell us that the new boyfriend turned out to be 'rotten like the rest.' Her identification with her mother frightens me.

Tina's happy when her mom's happy, sad when her mom's sad. But it infuriates me that Irene *tells* Tina the details of her love life, especially since her love life is so random and paints such a painful picture for her impressionable child."

Certainly, not *all* these stepmothers believe that their husbands' ex-wives are promiscuous, but many complain of a lack of shared values and morality between their homes and those of their stepchildren's mothers. Lacking common ground and mutual respect, women in the roles of "stepmother" and "mother" cannot help but clash. If the results are confusing to stepchildren, they are *maddening* to stepmothers.

Although they are committed to countering the influence of their stepchildren's mothers, most of these women have little direct contact with them. Usually, communication takes place indirectly, through the stepchildren or husbands. Many stepmothers prefer it this way, but the lack of direct communication leads some to take their frustrations out on the wrong people. Sometimes, too, the ex-wives use indirect communication as a method of manipulation or power.

"I rarely talk to Irene myself. I avoid her. I get so angry when I come face to face with her that my stomach literally has spasms. But, because her mother isn't around, I sometimes yell at Tina, even though I *know* that the problems aren't her fault. One Sunday, for example, Gordon and I planned to go to a five o'clock wedding. Irene agreed to pick up Tina at four. She didn't show up until after six. I was positively insane. Poor Tina. I spent two hours storming and ranting at *her* because her mother doesn't care about anyone but herself. I was so furious, I lost it completely."

These stepmothers, whether they hide their anger or display it, state that they feel they must compensate for the flaws of their stepchildren's mothers, "fix" their families and fill whatever needs anyone happens to have. Despite this heavy responsibility, they complain that they have no *voice* in their families. They have little contact with their husbands' ex-wives, face cool rejection by their stepchildren and are subject to the rigid instructions of their husbands. Overloaded externally and struggling internally, some give up and abandon their relationships with their stepchildren. Most, however, work to do their best by coming to terms with their own needs and limits, and balancing them against those of the other people in their families.

"I'm in a situation that has no apparent solution," Maxine concludes. "Irene *is* Tina's mother, and Tina naturally hungers for warmth and guidance from her. But Irene can't give those things. What she *does* give Tina are the details of her sordid romances, poor personal hygiene habits and unreliable promises about when she'll pick her up. Gordon wants me to provide Tina with what Irene can't. But Tina pushes me away, taking my 'mothering' efforts as put-downs of her mom. And I don't want to be a 'mother' to Tina. I simply want to be married to Gordon and to raise our little Ruthie in peace. Since that's too much to hope for, I hang in and try to do what I can."

Nobody's Buddy

Stepmothers whose stepchildren live with them often have unique relationships with the children's mothers. Some become quite close, sharing the role of "mother" and cooperating in the parenting process. More often, however, custodial stepmothers say that their stepchildren live with them because the mothers are unable, for various reasons, to provide the children with stable homes. Further, many find that the mothers often actively obstruct their efforts to form stable, close relationships with their stepchildren.

"The kids rarely find fault with Ann," Julie sighs. "They're supposed to visit her three out of every four weekends. But she *never* adheres to that schedule. She cancels at the last minute, or just doesn't show up. When the kids *do* see her, it's tough for me because they leave full of hugs and kisses and return two days later, barely speaking to me, blaming me for every problem their mother has. Ann tells them it's *my* fault she has no car. Who knows why? It's also my fault she has no money. Supposedly, *I* prevent their dad from giving her more. Every misery she has is somehow attributable to me. The kids buy it, every time, and it always takes two or three days of extreme effort and patience on my part to convince them that I'm *not* their mother's enemy."

Most stepmothers find that their stepchildren have extreme loyalty to their mothers, even when their experiences are marred by disappointment or pain. Sometimes, the stepchildren's mothers, angry and jealous, deliberately belittle stepmothers to the children. Other mothers' motives are even more ambitious, but generally more obvious than dangerous.

"One weekend," Julie remembers, "one of the kids left his homework at his mom's. Trevor couldn't go pick it up, so I went. Ann answered the door, expecting Trevor. She was real surprised to see me. She wore only a scant, low-cut bra and skimpy bikini pants. Sheer little things that were clearly *not* attire chosen to greet the *wife* of her ex-husband. When I remember the look of horror and embarrassment on her face when she opened the door, I simply laugh out loud."

For the most part, though, these women find that laughs are in short supply where their husbands' ex-wives are concerned. They find it difficult to plan their weekends because they don't know whether visitation schedules will be adhered to. They never know *what* stories the children's mothers will tell them, or what predicaments the ex-wives will call upon their former husbands to pull them out of. They find their own roles demanding, unappreciated, unsupported and often obstructed by their stepchildren's mothers. And they find themselves forever protecting their stepchildren from their mothers' inconsistent behavior.

"I neither like nor dislike Ann. I don't see Ann, actually, as a woman. I see her as a force that affects our family. A powerful, careless force, but one without bad intentions. Ann's dangerous, but she's not calculating. She's more like a loose cannon."

The greatest frustration of stepmothers like Julie is that they cannot attain equilibrium or peace for their families because their husbands' ex-wives prevent it. Even though they have custody of their stepchildren, they find it difficult or impossible to establish their own territory because the *title* of "mother" goes elsewhere, often with someone as inconsistent as the wind. Although they do not expect it, many hope that their stepchildren will see their mothers' and stepmothers' roles clearly, someday.

"Bottom line is that Ann *is* my stepchildren's mother," Julie says. "And that gives her the right to be with them. I know that. But the children have some rights, too. The right to stable, consistent interaction with her. The right to some caretaking. The right to a regular phone call, at least, when she lives in other cities. Instead, they get dinner every month or two when she breezes through town, empty promises, and plenty of time to dream fantastic dreams of her while she's away."

Compatibility and Respect

Many stepmothers actually *like* their husbands' ex-wives. Almost twenty percent even become friends with them.

These stepmothers are usually surprised at their fondness for the ex-wives. Most began their marriages avoiding contact with them, expecting friction and assuming that they would dislike each other. Many initially blamed the ex-wives for *everything* that was wrong with their marriages, husbands, finances or stepchildren. When they actually met and liked the ex-wives, they lost their scapegoats and were forced to reassess the causes of their own problems.

"In the beginning of our marriage," Jamie Simpkins recalls, "Keith was the one who dealt with his ex-wife, Patsy. I had virtually no communication with her. Keith handled all arrangements concerning Brittany. I had no sense of who Patsy was, except what I could guess at through my impressions of Brittany.

"And what I guessed wasn't very flattering. Brittany was spoiled, manipulative and possessive. If she didn't get what she wanted, she whined and moped all day. I blamed Patsy for this. I assumed her daughter mimicked her.

"Then, about four years into our marriage, I finally talked to Patsy. I answered the phone once when she called and, for some reason, I began to talk to her. Brit had been at her house all that week, and I knew she'd tried out for the school choir. I asked Patsy how Brit had done, and suddenly we were two women chatting as if we'd been friends for years. By asking her one simple question, I opened floodgates of communication. I'd somehow given her *permission* to talk to me. Apparently, she'd not known, until then, if I'd be comfortable talking with her, and she'd held back. She's a lovely person, really."

If they extend themselves to their stepchildren's mothers, some stepmothers find willing and friendly responses. When they realize that the mothers are not the witches they had pictured, they are forced to search for other reasons for their stepchildren's problems. Many find, as Jamie did, that these searches cause them to see their husbands more objectively and discover that much of the culpability for their stepchildren's problems lies within their own homes.

"After I got to know Patsy, my 'newlywed veil' was lifted and I began to see Keith's role in Brittany's behavior. Primarily, it was *his* guilt and insecurity that allowed, or actually *encouraged*, Brittany to be so demanding and manipulative. In fact, I discovered that Patsy was having the same sort of problems with Brittany that *I* was. By focusing on these problems together, we managed to begin a decent relationship *and* to be more effective in helping Brittany grow up."

Although they are generally fond of their stepchildren's mothers, these women find that they can become uncomfortable if they allow *too* much familiarity. They believe that their husbands are opposed to their becoming "too close" to the former wives, so they deliberately limit conversations to subjects related to their stepchildren or to neutral topics. At times, they find themselves somewhat confused or frustrated by these relationships, which *feel* like friendships, but, by their very natures and histories, are never quite true friendships.

"I've never told Keith that Patsy and I are such good buddies," Jamie declares. "I don't think Keith could handle his ex-wife and his wife being friends. He can barely stand to see me and his *daughter* talking. I know he'd go nuts if he thought Patsy and I were close."

Many of these stepmothers' husbands are unsure of themselves as postdivorce fathers and need to feel that they control their interactions with their ex-wives and children, even, sometimes, to the point of excluding their present wives from these relationships. Understanding this, these stepmothers do what they feel they must to keep their families functioning without unduly upsetting their husbands: they keep their relationships with the ex-wives secret, or at least out of sight.

"I don't tell George," one says, "that his ex and I share occasional recipes and thoughts. I don't want him to imagine that we *conspire* against him, or compare notes. It sounds like I'm sneaking around behind his back, but I actually feel like I'm protecting him from things he can't deal with."

Another elaborates, "It's not like I seek Tony's ex-wife out or that we're bosom buddies. We don't meet for lunch or play tennis. We have a nice relationship with only one safe topic between us. Occasionally, a related subject will come up, like a movie my stepkids have seen, and we'll start talking about movies. But when this happens, we both tread lightly, as if we're not sure it's okay for us to discuss anything other than the children."

In order to get along, these stepmothers and ex-wives follow definite, unspoken ground rules that actually go well beyond limiting their topics of conversation. First, the stepmothers respect the mothers' role. They neither want to be nor try to act like they are their stepchildren's mothers, and they limit themselves to trying to support *both* parents in their child-rearing efforts.

Next, the ex-wives and stepmothers carefully avoid rivalry and personal comparisons. They leave the events of the past alone, and look to each other as individuals, rather than as competitors. The ex-wives avoid references to their previous marriages, respecting the stepmothers' current role as "wife."

When these rules are followed, many stepmothers find that their relationships work so well that they wish they had met the ex-wives under different circumstances, so that they could have developed deeper and more natural friendships.

Helping Hands

Other stepmothers who rely heavily on their husbands' ex-wives and wish that their husbands were more comfortable about their relationships are those whose stepchildren have severe personal problems *requiring* the adults in their lives to communicate closely.

Jill Sterling describes how her stepson, Charlie, led her to discover his mother. "Ever since Charlie tried to hang himself, we've all become heavily involved in family therapy and intense communication. I know Ellen, Charlie's mother, and her new husband very well. I know more about Ellen's history with my husband than I care to because we all had to search together for the source of Charlie's problems. We have, the four of us, worked very hard to explore ourselves, our motivations, our relationships and their undercurrents, so that we can examine the impact we have on Charlie."

Stepmothers like Jill, whose families face life-threatening situations, find that barriers break down and pretenses are dropped. Personalities, roles and rivalries fade in the face of the crisis at hand. For Jill and Ellen, an instant partnership was formed because they *had* to participate in Charlie's "suicide watch." Others find that catastrophes like teenage pregnancy, serious illness or drug abuse draw stepparents and parents together to fight a common enemy far more menacing than each other.

Although these parents and stepmothers are all committed to

working together to help the children, the stepmothers think that their husbands are uneasy about their close relationships with their stepchildren's mothers.

"It makes Michael uncomfortable that Ellen, her husband, Tom, and I get along so well," Jill confides. "I'm positive that he'd like *not* to be in contact with Tom and Ellen, and, I think, if not for Charlie's crises and all the group therapy that's resulted, he might have resorted to sending messages home with Charlie, when necessary, thereby avoiding all direct communication."

These stepmothers are clear about their priorities: the well-being of their stepchildren comes first. Their own egos, rivalries with ex-wives, marital squabbles or other personal problems fall in line somewhere behind that. Because they are committed to helping their stepchildren survive major problems, they become effective members of their families' parenting teams, often developing strong alliances with, and deep appreciation for, the stepchildren's mothers. As allies, these mothers and stepmothers boost each other's spirits and refresh each other's perspectives. The stepmothers feel that the mothers appreciate their efforts to help their stepchildren and that they are sensitive to their conflicts in struggling with the crises of children who are not their own. In return, stepmothers give advice, understanding and support to mothers confronting their children's critical situations. At their best, these mothers and stepmothers form solid sisterhoods that help them *and* their families endure and, sometimes, overcome major hurdles.

"I know that many ex-wives and second wives have horror stories about each other. That's not true of us," Jill says. "For us, the horror comes from the emotional illness of a child, and we struggle to cope with that illness.

"Our situation, thank goodness, is *not* normal. We are, frankly, over our heads here. But I believe that Ellen is the glue that's allowed us all to stick together. She drives my husband nuts, but she keeps us focused on the issues, without blaming each other. I value and respect her. I've learned from her. I sincerely hope that she'd say the same about me."

Advice From Stepmothers on the Ex-Wife

1.   **Don't try to be a mother to your stepchildren.** Make it clear to them that your role does not conflict with their parents' roles. Make

it clear that you are an adult in the family, that you expect to be respected as such, that you are an individual and that your place in the family is different from that of either parent.

2. **Accept your stepchildren's mother as permanent.** Don't think she'll go away. As long as there are stepchildren, their mother will be part of your husband's—and, therefore, of your—life. Expect her influence over your stepchildren to be immense, no matter how little or how much contact you, your husband or the children have with her.

3. **Never speak ill of their mother to the children.** No matter how frustrated, indignant or justifiably angry you may be, never criticize their mother. If you must explain something negative to them, remember that she *is* their mother and that they have an entirely different relationship with, and image of her, than you do. Try to present your point of view without damaging their feelings of attachment and loyalty to their mother.

4. **Don't expect her to change.** Your husband's ex-wife is an adult, just as you are. She is who she is, like it or not. If you can't deal with her as she is, minimize your contact with her and discuss with your husband ways you can avoid having to relate to her.

5. **Have sympathy and a sense of humor.** Remember that it's probably as difficult for your husband's ex-wife to deal with you as it is for you to deal with her. If she drives you crazy, chances are you drive *her* crazy, too. Having to hand her children to you for visits, and seeing you happily married to their father is probably very stressful for her. Be patient.

6. **Try not to judge.** Remember, *your* family grew out of the remains of a failed marriage—there's a lot of history shared among the survivors of that marriage. Respect the status of the ex-wife and her right to a part of your husband's past. But, when you talk to her, keep the conversation on the issues at hand—don't let her bring up the past or raise her relationship with your husband. Make sure she respects your status as "wife" and "stepmother" as much as you do hers as "ex-wife" and "mother." Don't get into discussions with her that rightfully should be between her and your husband. And don't expose information to her that should stay within the province of your marriage.

7.   **Be yourself.** You didn't marry or divorce your husband's ex-wife. If you have trouble relating to her, don't feel that you have to fix it. Do what you can and leave the rest to your husband.

8.   **Don't become the middleman.** Don't allow yourself to be the messenger or buffer between your husband and his ex, or between the stepchildren and either parent. Do what you can to further direct, rather than triangular, communication.

9.   **Find out as much as you can *before* your wedding.** Talk to your husband about his relationship with his ex-wife, about her relationship with the children, about how he thinks she'll relate to you. If possible, meet her, talk to her about the children and the ways you can cooperate for their best interests. The more you learn *prior* to your wedding, the less you'll be surprised later.

10.   **Keep cool.** Be mature. Concentrate on enhancing your own marriage and family and the well-being of your stepchildren. Interact with your stepchildren's mother from that standpoint, and ignore everything else, especially anything that interferes with those goals.

11.   **Don't try to orchestrate your husband's relationship with his ex-wife.** Your husband and his ex-wife have a lot of history. He relates to her *his* way, and that may not be the way you wish he would. Don't bother to try to change their old patterns. He may act quite differently with her than he does with you. Remember, they couldn't work things out *during* their marriage; chances are, they won't be able to bring out the best in each other now that they're divorced. Leave their relationship to them, and concentrate on your own relationships in the family.

SIX

Coparenting

Coparenting, for stepmothers, involves a wide variety of parenting teams, levels of involvement and degrees of success. Often, stepmother, father, mother and stepfather work together in a cohesive parenting effort. Occasionally, though, stepmothers are unable to coparent effectively with one or more of the other adults. Sometimes, they work better with their stepchildren's *mothers* than with their own husbands. Many do not participate in the coparenting process at all.

One common reason that stepmothers do not participate is incompatibility of values between the stepmother and one or both of the parents. Another is the belief that it is not the stepmothers' "place" to help parent their stepchildren. Since their stepchildren's mothers and fathers are alive and well, many believe it would be presumptuous to interfere. Some, many years younger than their husbands, are their stepchildren's peers and would feel ridiculous "parenting" people who are in their own age group.

Stepmothers who *do* coparent encounter recurring patterns of intraparental alliance and opposition, such as stepfather/father against stepmother/mother, mother against father/stepmother, and mother/stepmother/stepfather against father.

A number of stepmothers, however, work easily with both parents, putting aside personal differences and coparenting according to shared long-term goals for the children.

Crisis Coparenting

Among the stepmothers who are deeply involved in coparenting and who work well with both parents are those whose stepchildren suffer from severe problems, such as drug abuse, physical handicaps or illnesses, or emotional disturbances. These stepmothers, drawn to the parents by crises, usually develop effective ways of working together for the children's sakes.

"For the most part," Jill Sterling says, "the four of us, my husband and I, his ex-wife and her husband, function compatibly as a team of parents for my stepson. I *wish* I could back out a little and concentrate more on my *own* children, but I can't. The reality is that I'm part of the 'Charlie team.' I'm *in*, whether I want to be or not. And, though I'm ambivalent about the *degree* of my involvement, I *care* about my stepson. I *do* want to have an influence. So, Charlie has four well-meaning, committed adults who work together, trying to 'parent' him back to normal life."

Stepmothers like Jill often meet with high levels of success in their coparenting efforts. They find that the adults *make* themselves get along, even when they disagree or get on each other's nerves, because the stakes are so high. They maintain constant communication, make joint decisions and closely examine any and all issues relevant to the stepchildren.

Even when all the adults are committed to the coparenting process, problems arise when there are differences of opinion about how to deal with a given issue. More than any other problem, stepmothers say that differences in values cause dissension among parents and stepparents. Sometimes, the values in question are relatively minor, concerning the importance of certain chores or privileges. Often, however, they concern fundamental issues like religion, goal-setting or respect for oneself or others.

"We get along, but we don't always agree," one stepmother says of her coparenting group. She believes that the death of her stepdaughter in a car accident has affected the way the rest of the family treats the surviving two boys.

"My husband's ex-wife, Gail, and her new husband are much more protective than we are. There are lots of inconsistencies, even though we try to minimize them. They don't allow the boys, who are twelve and ten, to go anywhere by themselves, even to the movies. They give the boys no responsibilities, not even cleaning up their rooms. But at *our* house they're expected to help out. And we try to give them some freedom, so they can learn how to manage on their own. We think it's wrong to keep them tied down. What happened to their sister is tragic, but it shouldn't be allowed to ruin *their* chances for normal lives."

Similarly, Jill says that her stepson's suicide attempt affected his parents' attitudes about his upbringing. "School is a big issue. Ellen and her husband, Tom, don't want to push Charlie. They want, at all costs, to keep stress down in his life. The result is that Charlie's a terrible underachiever. *C*'s are all his mom looks for, and so, *C*'s are what Charlie gives her. His mother's afraid to push because she thinks that *any* pressure on Charlie might drive him to try to kill himself again."

Although they share commitment with the other parenting adults, stepmothers like Jill often disagree with them on philosophy or technique. Their major frustrations are that they and their parenting partners are forever obstructing and countering each other's efforts, confusing already unbalanced or unhealthy children. Those who want to motivate their stepchildren, help them set goals and plan for adult life, are sometimes stifled by coparents who protect and coddle. Those who want to build their stepchildren's confidence by presenting them with escalating challenges are sometimes thwarted by coparents who want to minimize competition and stress.

"The result is that our coparenting team becomes like the proverbial committee that invented the camel," Jill says. "We have the best *intentions* and we respect each others' *motives*. But we can't agree on how to apply our intentions to reality. We *all* want Charlie to survive, thrive and be happy, but we have different ideas of how that should be achieved."

These involved stepmothers are concerned that the effects of too many committed parents can be almost as damaging as too few. They worry that the adults' disagreements will result in inconsistent, contradictory messages that prevent firm guidance. Often, they find that, as relative neutrals among the coparenting factions, they end up playing mediator.

"My husband gets very frustrated when he and his ex-wife disagree about his son," Jill explains. "He usually begins to lecture her. I'm sure he pushes the same buttons and uses the same condescending tone of voice that he did when they were married. She stiffens and won't even listen to him. So, in order to prevent *their* relationship from keeping us from making progress, *I* generally become the spokesperson for our point of view. Ellen has much less trouble dealing with me and listening to what I say, even if it's exactly what Michael has just said."

Some stepmothers find themselves preventing conflicts between fathers and *stepfathers*. "I like Flo's new husband," one stepmother comments. "But my husband thinks he's a 'wimp.' He says Bill's way too easy on the boys. Of course, my husband would think *any* man who doesn't eat nails for breakfast is a total wimp. But, joking aside, his attitude influences his sons. They blame their stepfather for everything that's wrong in their lives, even though Bill is far more patient, understanding, sensitive and tolerant than their father is. The boys idolize their father and berate their stepfather. I find myself taking their stepfather's side. It's somehow *my* job to see that all the parents are respected and taken seriously."

Overall, stepmothers of children in crisis believe they are effective coparents, working with other well-intentioned, caring adults. Although they cannot always resolve their differences, for the most part, they do *air* them. Their successes are due to cooperation that transcends relationships, personalities and interpersonal conflicts. At times, the coparenting adults get discouraged, tired and annoyed with each other. But, even at the worst times, they consider themselves part of a permanent team, devoted to the same goals.

"We're probably not going to get the parenting pennant," Jill quips, "but we're not striking out, either. If we keep at it, practice enough, who knows, maybe we'll make the all-stars. Or at least, as four adults, provide Charlie with something that approaches the kind of parenting he *should* have received from two."

Three's a Crowd

Stepmothers whose stepchildren live with them usually become heavily involved in coparenting whether they want to or not. Most work well with their husbands, but their effectiveness often depends on establishing their own authority and relationships with their step-children, independent of the natural parents. These independent relationships, however, must not conflict or compete with those of either parent.

"Trevor and I pretty much agree on how children should be raised," says Julie Sinclair. "We agree on curfews, allowances, what grades are acceptable, how old they should be when they begin to date. We also agree on discipline, or at least on what the limits of acceptable behavior are. Our conflicts aren't about what's right, but about how to react when things *aren't* right. And, maybe because I'm not the children's *real* parent, maybe *because* I'm a stepparent, I'm much more able to stay calm, cool and rational than Trevor is."

Like Julie, many stepmothers find that being a *step*parent allows them to coparent objectively and impartially. Their dealings with their stepchildren are less clouded by emotion, ego and identification than those of the natural parents, and their level-headed influence can greatly benefit their stepchildren.

"I rarely lose my temper with my stepchildren. It takes a lot for me even to raise my voice to them. Trevor, on the other hand, is so emotionally involved that, when they misbehave, he explodes. For instance, Kevin recently got a warning slip from school because he hadn't been doing his chemistry homework. I was home when the mail came, so I saw it first. I debated. Should I call Trevor at the office and ruin his day? Or should I let him find it after work, explode and ground Kevin for life? I decided to ruin his day. I called Trevor. Predictably, he yelled at me, since he couldn't yell at his son, and he told me I'd wrecked his entire day. When I told him I'd *chosen* to do that, rather than ruin the evening at home, he laughed and calmed down."

Like Julie, these stepmothers see one of their most important coparenting functions as providing some balance to their partner or partners. They recognize their partners' strengths and weaknesses and try to compensate for them. When a partner is out of patience or energy, or outnumbered by the stepchildren, they step in to reinforce him.

Although these stepmothers are able to work well with their husbands in coparenting teams, many find that family harmony completely disappears when a third coparent arrives: the mother. Whatever stability the custodial coparents have achieved can disinte-grate in the presence of visiting coparents who operate with different styles, goals and philosophies. Many stepmothers whose children live with them find that their stepchildren's mothers disrupt the delicate balance of their families because they are either unwilling or unable to cooperate in the coparenting effort.

"Every few months," Julie says, "a hurricane sweeps through our home. Hurricane Ann, Trevor's ex-wife, blows into our lives to assert her role of 'mother.' It's ludicrous to say that she's part of the parenting process, because what she does has nothing to do with what we do as parents. She's a non sequitur. There is nothing consistent in her interactions with her children. She enters and exits like a reckless gust of wind.

"For example, shortly after my stepson Zach got his driver's license, he was picked up for speeding. The next day, Zach called his mother and told her we'd taken his car privileges away. Ann instantly called Trevor in a rage. She was upset that Trevor was too strict with Zach. She thought that speeding was 'normal,' that 'all the kids' did it, and that we shouldn't be so tough on him just because he happened to get caught. She didn't perceive the need for consistency among parents, or Zach's need to learn respect, limits and responsibility. Zach needed to hear his mother back up the rules set by his father and the law. He heard no such thing."

Despite their differences in technique and philosophy, many stepmothers go out of their way to avoid conflicts with their stepchildren's mothers. Although their stepchildren live with them, they respect the differences between the roles of mother and stepmother, and they bend over backward to "make room for Mommy." Most stepmothers understand that their stepchildren love and accept their mothers, no matter how their mothers disappoint them. By contrast, they realize that, as stepmothers, they will forever have to *earn* their stepchildren's affection or friendship; love is not granted automatically to stepmothers, as it is to mothers.

"When we were first married," Julie recalls, "I *wanted* Ann to take part in the parenting. I thought we'd be better off if there were three adults raising Zach, Kevin and Tori. But Ann, even when she's in town, has no capacity for even the smallest part of parenting. She's never once taken one of her children to the dentist or soccer practice, never driven car pool. She's never even taken all three of them at once for an overnight visit. It's one child at a time for her, at her convenience, when she's in the mood. The fact that *I* have to care for *her* children, even when they're sick, or even when *I'm* sick or tired or in a bad mood, never occurs to her. There are times when I'd like to run off the way she does, believe me. But *I* could never do that to the kids."

Most stepmothers in situations like Julie's wish that they could participate in cooperative coparenting with their stepchildren's natural parents. They would prefer it if all the adults worked together and supported each other's efforts. For a variety of reasons, they find this impossible. Instead of a unified team of three, they find that their only chance is to team up two against one. But, fortunately for the team, that "one" is, usually, absent.

Stand-ins

Some stepmothers are willing to participate in coparenting, but find that their roles are unclear because their husbands are trying to eliminate unreliable, unstable ex-wives from the family scene. These fathers expect stepmothers to fill their ex-wives' places in the family, hoping to protect the children from being hurt or disappointed by their mothers. Accordingly, these stepmothers unintentionally, and often unwillingly, become competitors of their stepchildren's mothers. Their coparenting becomes a struggle to help raise their stepchildren while they counter the mothers' erratic behavior and fend off their husbands' unreasonable demands.

Maxine James believes that coparenting is actually impossible in her family because of the personality conflicts between the former spouses. "Irene, Tina's mother, cannot be counted on. You never know if she'll follow up on promises or forget them as soon as she makes them. It's usually small things, like Irene doesn't remember what time to pick Tina up, or she doesn't do the laundry, so Tina has to pack dirty clothes when she visits us. These issues may seem small, but they *are* important from Tina's point of view, because Tina sees herself as someone who isn't important enough for her own mother to bother about."

If stepmothers like Maxine are frustrated with the *mothers* of their stepchildren, they are absolutely bewildered about how to deal with the *fathers*. The fathers are so committed to providing their children with "good mothers" and stable homes that they attempt to recreate their original, predivorce families by erasing the actual mothers from the family and replacing them with the stepmothers. They try to deny the deep bond between mother and child and unrealistically try to force stepmothers into the role of mother. Ironically, their efforts often prevent stepmothers from establishing any meaningful role and sabotage their effectiveness as coparents.

Stepmothers in this situation feel that, in order to coparent, they have to overcome the pushy, overly zealous expectations of their husbands and clean up the messes, both emotional and physical, created by their stepchildren's irresponsible mothers. Even when they manage to work their way past the *parents'* obstacles, they often encounter resistance and suspicion from their *stepchildren*, who depend on them, but never admit it.

Women like Maxine are frustrated because, although they cannot work as an effective team with *either* parent, their stepchildren's well-being, in large part, depends on their parenting efforts. They understand their husbands' motives in trying to replace the children's mothers. They understand, too, their stepchildren's feelings that acceptance of their stepmothers would seem like rejection of their biological mothers. What these stepmothers have difficulty under-standing is the indifference of their stepchildren's mothers to the parenting process.

"Irene's only contribution to Tina's upbringing is to discuss money and logistics with Gordon. She never talks about Tina's performance in school, her friends or her overall development. Her conversations consist of excuses, arguments and requests for cash. She never seems to be aware of Tina, let alone concerned about her."

Overall, these stepmothers remain committed to the coparenting effort, despite the odds. They do not expect that their stepchildren's mothers will ever change, but they do hold onto hopes that, someday, their husbands will relax enough to allow them to develop their own relationships with their stepchildren and to become part of a mutually supportive coparenting team.

Although they are not acknowledged as such, many of these stepmothers are the central parenting figures in their stepchildren's lives. Because their husbands consistently want more from them, their stepchildren want less from them and the mothers simply want whatever they can *get* from them, they are often angry, resentful or hurt. Most, however, see their roles as too important to abandon, and continue to put their own needs aside, trying to please their husbands and appease their stepchildren.

No-Parenting

"Co-what?!" Jessie Solomon exclaims. "Co*parenting*?! Never! Is that too vague an answer? How about: No way! I'd want no *part* of it. I want *nothing* to do with Mark's ex-family. No co-mommying or co-babying, no co-*any*thing. That's why I waited to marry him until his kids were grown and gone. Coparenting? No. No thank you!"

While some stepmothers are completely immersed in coparenting, others refuse to enter into it at all. Some, like Jessie, find the idea repugnant because it would require them to tread across self-imposed borders into the realm of their husbands' previous marriages. They cannot bear to see their husbands' love for their children by former wives, to deal with those ex-wives or to acknowledge the history others share with their husbands.

Other stepmothers refuse to coparent because they don't want to face the effect divorce has had on their stepchildren. They have difficulty dealing with their *own* feelings about divorce and are afraid of discovering what might be hidden beneath their stepchildren's civil smiles. Many suspect that their stepchildren experience emotional conflicts similar to their own.

"I don't want to have to make up to them for whatever unpleasantness they've had to cope with," one stepmother explains. "My husband's children are *his* responsibility. I don't want to know how life has disappointed them, or how they've been damaged, or what they need from their parents. That bundle of problems is not something I want to take on."

Still other stepmothers refuse to coparent because they believe that the parenting of other people's children is neither their responsibility nor their prerogative. They see their role as an occasional hostess for their stepchildren, not as a loving, guiding or committed parental figures.

"Look," Jessie says, "'Coparenting' or 'parenting,' or however you say it, is the province of Mark and their mother, not me. It's between them. *I* didn't choose to bring my stepchildren into the world. Coparenting is not appropriate for me."

Whether because they believe that it is not their place or because they cannot bear to deal with their stepchildren's emotions, these women cut themselves off from the job of coparenting. In doing so, even if they try not to obstruct coparenting by the other adults, they risk harming their stepchildren and their husbands by appearing to abandon them.

Parents' Helper

Some stepmothers say that they do not "coparent," but that they are nevertheless very much involved with the upbringing of their step-children. They have humble, respectful attitudes toward parenting that prevent them from accepting a role as a parent.

"I'm not involved as a coparent," declares Molly Jerome. "The boys have two perfectly capable, healthy parents already. They don't need me or their stepfather to try to be parents, too. Frankly, I think it would be presumptuous on my part to think that my opinions or my values should determine how Ed and Rhonda raise their kids. I wasn't part of the decision to *have* the boys. I wasn't there when they were born or while they were infants or toddlers. I like the boys and want to have my own relationship with them, but it would be ridiculous for me to try to be *any* kind of *parent* to them."

In general, these stepmothers and their stepchildren's parents share basic values. When there *are* differences, they are usually about parenting style, rather than major issues. "At their mother's the boys don't have to do their homework before they watch TV. They don't have to help with dishes. But, at our house, TV is off until work is done. Meals are a family project. We all share in the preparation and cleanup. But even though the routines and expectations are different, both parents are consistent about *important* items, like honesty, sharing and love. It's not like she teaches them values that he abhors, or vice versa."

Stepmothers like Molly accept roles that are subordinate to both parents when it comes to raising their stepchildren. Even when they strongly disagree with the actions of one or both parents, they usually keep their opinions to themselves.

"Actually," Molly confides, "*I* think both Rhonda and Ed spoil the boys. I think my stepsons have no appreciation for all the material and emotional investments their parents make in them. But, as I've said, what I think is irrelevant to how they are raised. They're not my kids."

Occasionally, however, specific issues arise that concern these stepmothers enough that they feel compelled to express their opinions. When they do, they are careful to control what they say, how they say it and to whom. Although a few are comfortable discussing their stepchildren with the mothers, most direct their opinions to their husbands.

The stepmother's role, as women like Molly see it, is not to parent; rather, it is to *support* the parents and to be an extra, caring adult for the kids. They are there, *if* needed, *as* needed. Otherwise, they try to keep pleasantly low profiles. Molly sums it up: "When I'm wanted, I respond. And when I'm *not* wanted, I let them know that I'm still here for them, like a B-team. I don't make the headlines like their mom does. I don't get great pay. But the joy, when it comes—and it *does*, occasionally, pop up—is in playing the game, in having children in my life and in being part of their growing up."

Cut From the Team

"I don't even *see* my stepchildren, much less help *'parent'* them," Mia Jordan exclaims. "I never *talk* with their mother. I can't 'coparent' with her. Kate doesn't even allow their *father* to 'coparent.' Even though she's married again, she's a single parent, in that she's made sure that no other adult has anything to say about the children's upbringing. Kate is the *only* parent that Kate will tolerate. She makes all the decisions and sends Bob all the bills."

Like Mia, some women do not participate in coparenting because their stepchildren's mothers refuse to share parental authority with *anyone*. In these cases, when the fathers have little opportunity to take part in raising their children, stepmothers find that their chances of coparenting are nil. Most have little or no communication with their stepchildren's mothers. They and their husbands play no parts in the daily decisions concerning their stepchildren's lives. The mothers are completely in charge.

"Kate decides what camps the kids go to, what doctors they see, what vacations they take. She decides what activities they participate in, what chores they do. Occasionally, she sends Bob a note, along with a medical bill, telling him that Amy had a broken arm or that Nick had pneumonia. But that's *after* the fact, when it's too late for Bob to do anything."

Even when they have *some* communication with the mothers, these stepmothers say that neither they nor their husbands have any authority in dealings with the stepchildren. Whenever there is a dispute or a conflict in values, the mothers' opinions prevail. Many of these stepmothers feel more like babysitters than like equal partners in a coparenting effort.

These women are most frustrated when their stepchildren's mothers encourage values that conflict with their husbands' and their own. They are concerned about differing attitudes toward education, authority, religion, relationships, morals, communication and tolerance of others. In extreme situations, where one parent has tried to negate the presence, values and authority of the other, even the law is of little practical help.

"The values Kate sets up are subject to change, according to her mood and situation," Mia says. "The rules change with, and last for, the duration of Kate's whims. She even changes their *religions* at her fancy. She's made three changes of religious affiliation that we *know* of since the divorce, and we don't know *what* she's involved with now. Oh, Bob *could* go to court and defend his *right* to parent his children. He has the right to veto her religious cult activities and their retreats to so-called 'spiritual encounters.' But neither of us believe that court decisions really change what goes on inside the family, in private. In Nick's and Amy's home, no matter what the court decrees, Mother reigns. So there's no coparenting in our family, not even between the mother and father, and *certainly* not with me. None."

Spectators

Some stepmothers lack the authority to coparent because they are obstructed not by just *one*, but by *both* parents. They say that they play menial roles and do not take part in guidance, decision-making, discipline or limit-setting.

"It's not that I don't *want* to coparent," Jennifer Slade remarks. "I'd *love* it if my husband asked for my opinion, or if David's mother,

Gloria, wanted my advice. I'd be pleased and touched if my stepson, David, wanted my support or took me into his confidence. In fact, when David is with us and I see how close he and Alex are, I'm jealous. I'd *love* to be included in that."

Stepmothers who express frustrations similar to Jennifer's, feel excluded from the parent/child bond, from the bond between parents and, often, from forming their *own* bonds with their stepchildren.

"It's *my* job to cook the meals and change the sheets," one complains. "*I* clean the bathroom after Megan's visits. But *I'm* not part of the relationship she has with her dad. And Megan's mother makes no room for me on her end of things, either. She's barely civil to me. So I'm more like a maid than a coparent."

Many ex-wives dislike stepmothers so intensely that they refuse to converse, let alone coparent with them. Some blame stepmothers for their divorces; others clash in values and lifestyles so drastically that relationships are impossible to establish. Whatever the causes of their differences, stepmothers usually accept and eventually adjust to them. What continues to upset them, though, is that they cannot even assert authority with their stepchildren in their own homes.

"David follows his mother's rules, even at *our* house," Jennifer sighs. "I try to keep our home organized and orderly. We have a structured, regular routine. But when David's with us, he turns *our* lifestyle into Gloria's."

Although most husbands share stepmothers' displeasure with such behavior, some openly oppose them if they try to assert parental authority. Stepmothers in this situation describe themselves as "timid," "chicken" and "walking on eggshells" around their stepchildren. They feel excluded not only from the coparenting process, but also from equal status as members of their stepfamilies. Although they are envious of the intimacies enjoyed by their stepchildren and their parents, they are so afraid of losing that they will not risk confrontations that might improve their situations. They see their stepchildren as barriers to their husbands, their husbands as barriers to their stepchildren's mothers, the mothers and husbands as barriers to their stepchildren. No matter which relationships they focus on, they see themselves as outsiders looking in, without either the hope of being invited or the power to enter on their own.

"I wouldn't call this 'coparenting,' would you? Not when I can't talk to either parent about their son. Not when David lies on my new sofa with his shoes on and I don't dare say anything. Not when I can't tell him to turn off the TV, even at dinner or bedtime. Not when I lose my husband whenever my stepson's around. There must be a name for my situation, but it's not 'coparenting.' I'm sure of that."

Team Manager

Some stepmothers, however, are the pivotal figures around whom *all* family interaction, including parenting, takes place. The parents as well as the stepchildren in their stepfamilies depend on them as vehicles for communication and buffers for emotions. Without these stepmothers, family members have trouble dealing with each other. As relatively impartial newcomers, the stepmothers become messengers, confidants, interpreters and, sometimes, referees.

Maggie Joyner doesn't think of herself as a coparent. "It's more like I'm a funnel through which his parents' parenting reaches Josh. I end up in the middle. Everybody talks through me. When Brad wants to talk to Maria, when Maria wants to talk to Brad, when Maria's new husband wants to talk to Brad or Josh, when either parent wants to talk to Josh or when Josh has a matter to take up with either parent— whenever there's a message to be made, everybody comes to Maggie. I feel like a communications center."

In addition to communication, many like Maggie provide the structure for their families. They found that their stepchildren's parents were, by themselves, unable to set limits or establish routines. Discipline, prior to their arrival in the family, was unenforced or unpredictable. Their stepchildren often suffered from their parents' vagueness and apparent indifference; many developed severe behavioral or emotional problems and, as teenagers, several became involved in alcohol and drugs. Even though these stepmothers are much stricter and more demanding than the parents, their stepchildren relate to them well and appear to relax under their supervision.

"My rules get followed or there are consequences," Maggie says. "Josh knows that and behaves much better with me than with his parents. He needs to know what the rules are. And, since I'm not blinded by emotions the way his parents are, it's easier for me to tell him what's appropriate and what's not where his behavior is concerned."

Stepmothers like Maggie define their roles as precisely as they would professional job descriptions. They separate their responsibilities from their emotions, intending to be fully accountable for the impact they have on their stepchildren. They strive to be coolly objective and controlled, even when they are tired, pressured or upset. Because they see their stepchildren's parents as inconsistent, they compensate by being consistent to a fault, warning parents when they observe them repeating old, destructive patterns.

Further, as the primary vehicles of communication for their stepfamilies, women in situations like Maggie's are often awkwardly thrust into the relationships of their stepchildren's parents. They review marital and postdivorce histories, identify behavior patterns and their effects on the stepchildren and analyze everyone's underlying motives and feelings. Sometimes, they even try to initiate change, going so far as to suggest that the entire family participate in therapy.

"Josh's parents, Brad and Maria, always undermine each other. They blame each other for everything, right in front of Josh. But neither of them holds *Josh* accountable for *Josh's* behavior. When Josh broke a china vase, it was Maria's fault for leaving the vase on the table and Brad's fault for letting him play cops and robbers. When Josh, at age twelve, took his dad's car and smashed it into a parked van, it was Brad's fault for leaving the keys around and Maria's fault for not watching Josh closely enough. Nothing was ever Josh's fault!

"I've tried to show them that they've used Josh's behavior as their battleground. I try to show them how I see him: an overgrown little boy who broke a window and is waiting to face the consequences, only to see his parents baring their teeth and punishing each other, while *he* sits forgotten on the sidelines."

Women like Maggie know that they cannot undo the damage of the past or solve all their families' problems. They are, however, steadfast in their determination to try to "be there" for their stepchildren and to help the parents communicate so that, someday, the entire family can stop hurting itself and begin to heal.

"Meantime, my stepson leans on *me* because he knows where I stand, and so I'm going to keep on standing here. I'm here, hoping, for Josh's sake and ours, that we four adults can get it together to 'coparent' him before he's too old and it's too late."

Face-off

Although some stepmothers do participate in coparenting, they are locked into battles with their stepchildren's mothers. They find their efforts primarily aimed at fighting the mothers, especially where intangibles like morals, ethics and values are concerned.

Marla Jenson declares, "It's never been *co*parenting. It's been *separate* parenting. Without discussing or acknowledging it, we've been involved in a silent battle of wills that's lasted almost nine years."

Although they try to be involved in coparenting teams, these stepmothers act alone because their husbands are unwilling to get involved in conflicts between them and the ex-wives. In fact, the men would rather do *anything* to placate both women than to take a side in their fight. Many of the husbands, for whatever reason, will not stand up to their ex-wives.

"During their marriage, and even in their divorce settlement, Steve gave Pam whatever she wanted. It's always been easier for Steve to give in than to argue with her. But now it's different. Now, Pam has to reckon with *me*."

Most of these women disagree with their stepchildren's mothers on issues like education, money management, discipline and levels of responsibility delegated to the stepchildren. They call the mothers' values "irresponsible," "undisciplined" and "self-indulgent," and do not hesitate to oppose them openly, even if it means putting their husbands in the middle.

"When Steve began to live with me," Marla says, "he became torn between two value systems, trying to appease two women who demanded different, at times opposing, responses from him regarding the children, Tiffany and Eric. I believe in discipline, rules, structure and earning rewards through hard work. Pam believes, simply, in having Steve pay for everything the kids want and buying them out of whatever trouble they get into."

Stepmothers like Marla are generally strong-willed and outspoken, but they find themselves up against long histories and patterns that are hard to break. Some, whose stepchildren are not much younger than *they* are, find that their stepfamilies do not take their opinions about coparenting seriously. Others often discover that their husbands, the ex-wives and the stepchildren are comfortable with existing values and interaction patterns. As newcomers to the family, they stand alone in their desire for everyone to change and follow new rules.

Because even their husbands are reluctant to change old habits, set limits or establish new rules, these women find that they must set modified, more realistic goals if they are to accomplish anything in coparenting their stepchildren. Most eventually give up trying to change the values, goals and behavior of the other family members. Instead, they minimize contact with their stepchildren's mothers and content themselves with controlling their own homes and assets. Most believe that their influence as coparents is minimal, but they feel that it is important to reinforce their positions, in the remote chance that they may have *some* effect on their stepchildren. Some, however, gradually begin to wonder whether they should even bother to remain involved.

"The way I've dealt with this battle of wills, after years of frustration, is that *I* set rules in *our* house. But I don't try, anymore, to change their mother or to argue with her about what kind of mother she is. I stay out of her path. If Steve wants to talk to her that's *his* business. I don't want to get involved in any more disputes, or watch Steve be bullied by his ex-wife. I just take care of my own territory. It may be too late to undo what my stepchildren's mother has done and their father has allowed. And, I'm not sure, anymore, that it's my job to try. I still believe in the same values, but, in reality, it's tough to overrule *any* kid's mother, as far as the kid's concerned."

Surprisingly, changes sometimes occur for these stepmothers when their grown stepchildren announce their engagements or marry. When the mothers confront the prospect of *in-laws*, they sometimes cease fire and seek alliances with the stepmothers. Some of the mothers, in fact, become so shaken by their children's marital choices that they accept the stepmothers as their confidants and coconspirators against the dreaded intended unions.

"It *was* true that the family was barbaric," one stepmother remarks. "They had abominable table manners. We took them out to dinner and they complained loudly about everything from the decor to the dessert. They said, in so many words, that we should have taken them someplace more expensive. Nothing we did was good enough for them. By comparison, they made *me* look *good* to my husband's ex-wife, Margo, who's always hated me. She called me to commiserate and we ended up laughing together about how awful the fiancé was. Eventually, the engagement was broken off by the young man, and, together, we've helped nurse my stepdaughter's broken heart while secretly sharing joyous relief. Our relationship has reversed. We're *almost* friends, now."

When faced with a common enemy, the differences over which coparents battle seem slight. Traumatic events, like disappointing engagements or unhappy romances, frequently allow stepmothers and their stepchildren's adversarial mothers to see each other and their values in a different light. Former enemies sometimes gain the ability to form a unified, if belated, coparenting team, of sorts.

One-on-One-on-One

Jamie Simpkins grins when she discusses coparenting. "Brittany has three adults to parent her and that makes, let's see, three sets of parenting teams of two, plus a fourth team of one, since her father considers himself a 'parent' unto himself."

Jamie is one of many stepmothers who work well as a team with either parent, but only one at a time. They pair off because they cannot get along, let alone parent effectively, in groups larger than two.

These women believe that their husbands create the main obstacles to their family's coparenting. Some husbands try to block communication between their wives and ex-wives because they are uncomfortable about mixing their past with the present, even for their children's benefit. Others are reluctant to let *anyone* participate in their relationships with their children; they need to feel that these relationships are sacred spheres into which *no one* can intrude. Stepmothers and mothers in these situations struggle to work around the husbands' limits and conditions to develop successful coparenting teams.

Many of these women admit that their husbands' limitations have been difficult or even painful for them. Some feel excluded and rejected when their husbands refuse to include them in parenting decisions and activities. Others become jealous of their stepchildren because they feel that the children get the best part of their husbands' attention and affection. Eventually, though, most come to understand that their husbands do not necessarily *want* to exclude them or to favor their children; rather, they parent independently because they are incapable, for a variety of reasons, of focusing on more than one relationship at a time.

"In the beginning of my marriage, I was jealous of my stepdaughter. I thought Brittany monopolized Keith, that she deliberately took all his time and attention. As time went on, I got to know my husband better, and I realized that *he* was the one doing the monopolizing. Keith was afraid of losing Brittany's affection, guilty about hurting her when he divorced Patsy, trying to hold on to her by indulging her. When I married Keith, I *wanted* to coparent with him. But the only real 'team' Keith could participate in was one in which I was his flunky, following orders and taking a backseat to my stepchild. *That* got old *real* fast."

Many of these stepmothers discover that they have more success coparenting with their husbands' ex-wives than with their husbands, often teaming up with them to prevent or overrule situations they oppose. They reinforce each other's limits and rules, so that the stepchildren experience consistency in both their mothers' and their fathers' homes. Among other skills, their roles require timing, psychology and diplomacy.

"I remember one time when Patsy called me to say that Brittany had asked her to buy her a sweater that was outrageously expensive. Patsy had said no, that they couldn't afford it. Brit was coming to our house that weekend, and Patsy predicted that Brit would ask Keith for the sweater, and that, as usual, Keith would indulge her.

"When Patsy told me this, I knew that I'd have to intervene if we were to keep our rules consistent. But time was of the essence. If Brit asked Keith for the sweater *before* I got to her, Keith would resent my interference and overrule me. So, when Brit arrived, I took her aside and told her that Patsy had mentioned the neat sweater she'd wanted and that it was a shame it was so expensive, since it sounded exquisite. I was careful not to say, 'Don't ask your father to buy it,' or, '*I* know your mother already said you couldn't get it.' I didn't want to make her mother sound like a tattletale, and I didn't want to appear to be coming between Brit and her father. But I *did* want to back Patsy up and support her decision, so Brit would know that there was agreement between our house and Patsy's as to limits. It worked. She didn't mention the sweater to her father."

Stepmothers like Jamie are often caught between their stepchildren's parents. While they do not feel *disloyal* to their husbands, they do try to "keep a lid on" what their husbands do for their stepchildren, so that the stepchildren will not play one parent against another. More than any other single factor, consistency is important to their stepchildren's upbringing, and they strive to achieve it for them. In order to do that, they build whatever parenting alliances and networks they can.

"Patsy and I are a mother and a stepmother who are trying to raise a child in the best way possible within the realities of our family situations," Jamie explains. "Keith is a father who dotes on his daughter, and his adoration sometimes colors his judgment. So, we work around him, when we have to, and we *aren't* above ganging up on him when it's important," she laughs.

Most of these stepmothers get along amicably with the other coparenting adults, but are careful to observe the invisible lines that divide the "parenting pairs." Although they may act as transmitters or translators, they are careful not to repeat conversations they have with their husbands to the ex-wives, or those they have with the ex-wives to their husbands. They respect the territory of their stepchildren's parents and the personal relationships of former spouses.

"Patsy complains a lot to Keith about spoiling Brit or being too lenient. Keith tells Patsy she's too strict and rigid about rules. I stay out of these spats. They belong to the parenting team of Patsy and Keith and contain a lot of leftover emotions from their marriage. To intervene would be an intrusion. They bicker, and the bickering often focuses on Brit. But, as long as it doesn't get out of hand, I stay out of it."

These coparenting teams of two are often quite effective, in part because it is easier to work and communicate with one adult at a time than with a "committee." Over time, most of these stepmothers feel satisfied with the results of their efforts. Although some lament their husbands' inabilities to relax about their coparenting roles, they feel pleased with the way their coparenting methods accommodate reality.

"Despite her three separate parenting teams and her independent, doting father, Brittany has turned out, at sixteen, to be a charming, attractive young woman. She's mature enough now to need very little coparenting. We're here as advisors on an as needed basis. All of us enjoy her company, her humor and her spirit. And, if we ever could manage to be together long enough, we'd deserve to pat each other on the back because, for all our difficulty in cooperating and coparenting, we've done *something* right! All we have to do is look at Brit to see proof of that!"

Advice From Stepmothers on Coparenting

1.   **Do what you can, within your own limits.** Successful coparenting requires the commitment and cooperation of several adults, not just the stepmother. If one or more of your stepchildren's parents fails to participate, it's not your fault. Worse, if one or more parents *oppose* coparenting, even your best efforts are probably doomed. Be as involved or as uninvolved in the parenting process as *you* choose to be, given your particular relationships, feelings and stepchildren's needs.

2.   **Communicate carefully.** Coparenting involves the effort, patience and understanding of several adults whose own relationships can be quite complicated and even unpleasant. It's often important to keep communication limited to topics directly relevant to the children, and to make sure you stay on the subject at hand. If you are uncomfortable with the other coparents, don't allow conversations to go off in directions that are unrelated to your stepchildren's concerns or interests.

3.   **Keep the children in mind.** The whole point of coparenting is the best interests of the children. It isn't necessary to like or be friends with the other adults involved. Try to be tolerant of the other adults, so that you can accomplish your goals for your stepchildren.

4.   **Listen.** It's important to understand the feelings and perceptions of the other coparents, even if you don't agree with their points of view.

5.   **Compromise.** Be willing to bend a little, at least on issues that are relatively minor. Consistency among parents' rules can be more important to children than the actual rules themselves. Children benefit from knowing that their parents are in agreement.

6.   **Don't put the kids in the middle.** Even when the children's

mother or stepfather is unreasonable or undependable, don't speak ill of either of them to your stepchildren. The children's mother *is* their mother; she merits their respect. If necessary, provide an alternate, more satisfactory 'mothering' model for them, but don't try to belittle or discredit her or her new husband, if she has one. Talk to your husband and to the other coparents about problems, not to the kids. Don't compete with the other coparents for the children's affections or loyalties. Remember that you *all* share the same goals for the children; put these goals first.

7.   **Be flexible.** Depending on the personalities and dynamics involved in your particular situation, you may have to adopt any number of roles. You may be the middleman between ex-spouses, or the funnel through which frustrated parents reach out to their children. In coparenting, identify the role that the children *need* you to fill, that the other coparents cannot fill, and that you are capable of and comfortable with. Remember, it's not your job to fill *all* the roles, or to be the answer to *all* your stepchildren's problems. But you *will* be most effective if your work *with* the other adults, supporting their strengths and compensating for their weaknesses.

SEVEN

Your Kids, My Kids, Our Kids...

Eighty percent of the stepmothers we interviewed have children of their own. More than seventy-five percent of these have children from their present marriages, twenty percent have children from prior marriages and about ten percent have children from both marriages. Overall, we found that stepchildren outnumber the stepmothers' own children by two to one and, at the average age of seventeen, stepchildren are usually three years older than their stepsiblings from the stepmothers' prior marriages and thirteen years older than their half siblings from the present marriages.

Most stepmothers put their predominant focus on their *own* roles and relationships with their natural and stepchildren. They are primarily concerned with how well they themselves meet the needs of the various children, how they feel about them and whether they favor some over others. They are also concerned about the roles of their husbands and the relationships among stepsiblings.

The majority find that the relationships that develop between their own children and their stepchildren seem easier and more peaceful than those between natural siblings. The success of these relationships may be due, in part, to the children's age differences, which minimize

139

rivalry and competition. In these families, stepmothers say that their younger children are treated like "pets" or "china dolls" by their stepchildren. Other stepmothers, however, see relations between their own and their stepchildren as less harmonious than those among natural siblings, and view the interaction as "destructive," "harmful" or "dangerous."

Although many stepmothers think that their husbands favor their stepchildren, most see their husbands as better fathers to *their* children than to their stepchildren. They attribute this improvement to age, maturity, objectivity and, most of all, to their happy marriages.

Even when these husbands are dedicated to home and family, however, many have difficulty combining the roles of father to the children of two marriages. As a result, fathers "divide" themselves between the two young groups of children and behave quite differently with each. Even though their husbands have grown and matured, many stepmothers discover that their stepchildren's old expectations, roles and interaction patterns are hard to change.

His, Hers and Theirs

"Danny is *mine*, Brittany is *his*, Stuart is *ours*. It's confusing to *me*, so I can imagine that it's confusing to other people!" Jamie Simpkins laughs. Her family includes three types of children: his, hers and theirs.

Though it takes time, families like Jamie's usually achieve steady, positive relationships. Even so, stepmothers in this situation experience major differences between their roles as mothers and stepmothers, and many feel more effective and consistent as stepmothers. As stepmothers, they are able to provide rational, logical, carefully considered advice and guidance. As mothers, they often find it difficult to separate enough emotionally to be objective or think clearly, especially in times of stress.

"I talk to my stepdaughter from my 'head,'" Jamie says. "But I talk to my *own* kids purely from my heart and guts. When my sons have a problem, *I* have a problem because I'm so close to them.

"Last year, for example, Brittany had trouble with one of her teachers. I advised her to make an appointment to talk with him privately, and we spent hours making a list of questions for the teacher so that she could learn exactly how to improve things. She discovered that the teacher was being deliberately tough on her, so she would try harder for A's instead of being lazy with B's. She felt good after the talk, and so did I, for helping her.

"Not two weeks later, my son Danny came home with a similar story of a teacher who was 'picking' on him. This time, I didn't ask questions or wait to hear details. My heart pounded and my adrenaline flowed. I called the school immediately and told off the principal, who connected me with the teacher, who finally stopped me cold by telling me the facts. Danny, it seems, had been wearing a cap in class and refusing to remove it. He'd been loud, disruptive and rude to the teacher. Because I hadn't questioned Danny about *why* the teacher was 'picking' on him, I'd no idea whether the teacher's charges were true and, therefore, had no answers for her. In fact, I had nothing to say except to apologize for losing my temper and back off foolishly, mumbling amenities."

Although they recognize the contrasts in their behavior, these women usually find that the relationships between their children and stepchildren are unaffected. One stepmother is amazed at how well her teenager from a prior marriage, her four-year-old from this marriage and her husband's sixteen-year-old son get along. "The kids seem to have a real family-type bond or loyalty. My son was in a contest to see who could sell the most magazines and my stepson told his mother *he* was in the contest so she and her friends would buy some. My stepson sold eleven subscriptions for my son! They were a team. They like each other and don't seem to compete the way 'real' brothers might."

If the rivalries typical to siblings are mitigated in these families, it may be because the children do not compete for the attention of the same sets of parents. These children and stepchildren get along with each other better than siblings in nuclear, 'non-step' families, where there are just one female and one male adult for the children to share. Even so, *some* tensions among the children are inevitable.

"Believe me, this is *not* Camelot," Jamie declares. "The kids fight. They can be real rough with each other. Sometimes there are screaming fights that target the adults: 'Your father's a creep!' 'Oh yeah? Your mother's a pig!' 'Well yours is a dork just like *you* are!' It's actually comical, because I have to stop and think just which mother they're talking about, and if they're taking *my* name in vain, well, you bet I stop the argument!"

These women do not pretend that their stepfamilies have all the answers. Overall, though, they are convinced that the children understand and accept the differences that exist in their families—the kids do not *expect* their stepparents and parents to relate to them the same ways. And, although these stepmothers admit to inconsistencies and even some favoritism, they believe that their stepfamilies are strong, cohesive and durable. They see room for improvement, but speak of both their children and stepchildren with positive attitudes and affection.

Jamie sums it up. "We're a patchwork. We're not blended. We're attached, but we're connected to each other seam by seam. The bonds between parent and child are different than those between stepparent and stepchild. The ones between siblings are different than those between stepsiblings. I think we're successful, though. At least, we can usually remember who's related to whom and how."

A Kid Is Just a Kid

A fifth of the stepmothers we interviewed were childless. Most had no children because their careers had come first, because they had not wanted children or because the opportunity had never presented itself until now, when it was "too late." Almost half would like to have children, but their *husbands* would not. Most of the others were incapable of bearing children. Whatever prevented them from being mothers, most had strong opinions about how their relationships with their stepchildren might have compared to those with children of their own.

Some childless stepmothers maintain that they would feel no differently about their *own* children than they do about their stepchildren. Molly Jerome is among them.

"I love children and I need to have them in my life. When I found out I couldn't have children, I decided to adopt. You don't have to give birth to a child to love him or her. But then I met Ed, who already *had* two kids and didn't want more. So, emotionally, I adopted my stepsons. They are the children in my life."

Although these women concentrate their maternal energies on their stepchildren, they are careful to remember that they are *not* their stepchildren's mothers and that their roles *are* different than that of "parent." Some establish close relationships and are content with contributing to their stepchildren's growth and development. Many, however, find that their stepchildren are too conflicted about them to accept their influence. Like Molly, most hope that, eventually, their good intentions and fondness for the stepchildren will prevail.

"I can wait," Molly sighs. "There's no rush. I don't want the boys to do or be anything that isn't honest for them. I give what I give because I *want* to, not so I'll get anything *back*."

Unlike Molly, some stepmothers were devastated that they would never have their own children. And for these women, even stepchildren who resist them are better than no children at all.

"Even with our 'ups and downs,'" one remarks, "the kids give me more than I can *ever* give them. I'm refreshed by their energy and their eagerness for life. I don't have to be their 'mother' to be affected by that, or to witness the magic and innocence of their youth, or to try to encourage them to 'follow their stars.' Even if they never give a hoot about me, they've given me treasures I'd have sorely missed without them."

Although most of these childless stepmothers are prepared to love their stepchildren as their own and believe that they enrich their lives, a few admit to unresolved feelings about the children they will never have. At times, especially when they feel discouraged or tired, questions arise that they cannot answer.

"Sometimes I wonder," Molly says, wistfully. "Maybe it *would* have been different to have my *own* child. How would it *feel* to actually *be* 'Mom.' I'll never know. What I've got is what I've got, and it's just fine. Even better than fine. At least," she laughs, "it's never dull!"

Waiting for Her Own

Others who are childless still hope to have children. Most expect that it will be very different to raise their own children; they just don't know *how* different. They discuss "bonding" and genetic links, express wonder that their love for their husbands might emerge in the form of a new human being. But the greatest differences they anticipate between their own and their stepchildren have little to do with either biology or romance.

"I'll *meet* my child the day it's *born,*" Maggie Joyner beams. "The very *instant* it's born. That's a *lot* earlier in life than when I met my stepson. By the time I met Josh, he was a teenager and a *mess*! He'd been thrown out of school and was hooked on drugs, down on himself and totally undisciplined. I came on the scene too late to do much good."

Although not all of their stepchildren share Josh's problems, most of these stepmothers are very involved in their upbringing and development, and many worry about the effects the birth of their own children will have on their stepchildren.

"I wonder if my feelings will change when we have our own baby," Maggie confides. "I devote a lot of time and energy to Josh, and I worry that I'll resent him for taking time away from the baby. But sometimes I wonder if I'll resent the baby for taking so much time away from Josh! Or from my husband and my life as I know it. Friends tell me that just about all women who have children later in life have similar worries, though. And so do women who are having a second child.

"One thing that will be different, though, is that I will not have to define my 'step' limits all the time. I'll be free to be *Mom*! I'll be able to be there from day one, to cuddle, kiss, sing silly songs, make faces and tell bedtime stories, without worrying that I'm invading someone else's turf. *I'll* be the one to listen, encourage and guide my child through the first years of life, to help him or her get a good start."

Another stepmother, four months pregnant, adds, "I don't know what I'm in for," she says. "But I *do* know that the new baby will take endless time, emotion and energy. And it will be nice to give all those things to my *own* child, instead of to someone else's."

He Has, She Has Not

Stepmothers who have no children because of their husbands' decisions often find that having stepchildren provides little consolation for their frustrated maternal instincts. Although they have readjusted their expectations of life and marriage, many confess that giving up the hope of becoming mothers took years.

Jennifer Slade adjusted only by teaching herself to dream different dreams. "My new dreams included undying romance in my marriage, and the freedom to travel with my husband, cook gourmet dinners and cuddle by the fireplace, uninterrupted by diaper changes and toddler tears. Unfortunately, reality and my dreams are quite different. I don't have a child, but neither do I have the marriage I'd envisioned. Instead, I have my stepson, David."

Women like Jennifer speak about their childlessness and their compromises with little bitterness. They consciously chose to marry men who already had children and who clearly did not want more. But, despite their knowing choices, many are plagued by ambivalence. Although they knew that they would have stepchildren, rather than children, in their lives, they did not know what that would mean. Many regret abiding by their husbands' wishes and are angry that their husbands enjoy fatherhood while denying them the experience of motherhood.

"I still wish, deep down, that I could have a child," one confesses. "There's a painful void in my life. I try not to dwell on it and never mention it to my husband, but there it is. I've said it."

Many believe that their status in the family would change dramatically if they had a child. Jennifer muses, "I wouldn't need as much from my husband or my stepson. I wouldn't be as vulnerable or jealous of their relationship, because I'd have my *own* child. I'm certain that I'd feel more sure of myself in the family, more of an equal with my husband and under less pressure to please everyone. It's useless to dwell on these ideas, but they arise from time to time."

These stepmothers find that *some* tensions exist in their marriages simply because their husbands do not share their desire to have children. These tensions, however, are often multiplied because the stepmothers are left craving the sort of relationships that their husbands already have, and sometimes appear to flaunt. Even when they get along with their stepchildren, they find no relief from their own yearnings.

"Sometimes when we're having a good time," Jennifer says, "I'm overcome with an awful sadness, as if being close to David reminds me of my own personal loss. And I get jealous of the intimacy between Alex and David, that only a parent and child can share. My marriage is affected. If not for David, my husband *would* have wanted to have a child with me. Instead, he's David's parent, so David is constantly present in our lives. I get neither the freedom nor the romance that I'd hoped might ease the pain of not having my own child. I try to do my best. But I remain, in a very basic way, the outsider in the family, the one who's not, and never will be, a branch on the family tree."

His and Theirs

For some stepmothers who are also mothers, there is a huge, basic difference in their relationships with their own children and their stepchildren, a difference that is strictly emotional. Marla Jenson explains, "Look, I *love* my daughter. I don't even *like* my stepchildren."

Many like Marla attribute the difference to the children's relative ages. Their own children are younger, more dependent and more impressionable than their stepchildren. The older the stepchildren, the more stepmothers expect of them and, often, the more they are disappointed.

"I expect different things of my stepchildren at ages twenty-two and twenty-six than I expect of my seven-year-old," Marla explains. "I expect Sara to behave like a child. I expect *them* to behave like adults. I expect them to be respectful to their father and friendly to their half sister, to be responsible for their expenses, to help clear the table when they eat here. Things like that. But they don't. They act like overgrown, selfish, spoiled brats."

Many of these women see their own children in terms of developmental stages and in the context of life events, but they are unaware of their stepchildren's early life experiences and find it difficult to explain or interpret much of their behavior.

"I didn't know them as babies or as children," Marla says. "I see them only as they are, not as they used to be. I see very demanding, needy adults, not the children that my husband sees. They may have the emotional makeup and needs of children, but I don't want to get into that with them. Their arrested developments and limited emotional capacities are not my problem. I just want them to act like adults."

Women like Marla find it difficult to tolerate the way their husbands parent their stepchildren and insist that their own children be raised with more structure. The fundamental difference is choice. They feel that it is their prerogative to select the kinds of relationships they have with their stepchildren. Unlike their own children, their stepchildren must earn a place in their lives.

Theirs Without His

"My stepchildren hate me," one stepmother explains. "My own children love me. I react differently to love than to hate."

Some women's feelings for their own and their stepchildren merely mirror the children's feelings for them. They claim that they are not responsible for the enormous differences that exist in their relationships with the two groups of children because the children themselves determine what develops. In fact, for many, the nature of their steprelationships is so far beyond their control that they have lost all contact with their stepchildren.

One woman who struggled to treat her stepchildren no differently from her own met with constant rebuffs. "If I even tried to touch them, to give a hug or a pat, my stepson would recoil, my stepdaughter stiffen. We just didn't know how to conduct a relationship. It's not like a mother and her kids, who just naturally bond. My stepchildren and I were thrown together without common blood or common goals. They were cold and distant and I never knew how to approach them."

Some stepmothers better understand this rejection after they have children of their own. Mia Jordan states, "I am drawn to my own children in a primal way. I feel closely connected to them. But I've never felt *any* link whatsoever to Nick or Amy." For women like Mia, the difference in their feelings is not simply the result of giving birth to children. They emphasize that the difference comes from the children's own openness, or lack of it.

Mia explains, "My kids have always looked at me lovingly, with trust, acceptance and, often, joy. But Nick and Amy have *always* been guarded and negative, even hostile. I don't know how to react."

Many women in this situation are concerned about the relationships between their own children and their older, rejecting stepchildren. Even in families untouched by divorce, many older siblings resent younger ones. However, the conflicts among half and stepsiblings can be even more complicated because of their families' histories. Often, stepmothers find that their own children take the brunt of these step-conflicts. Lacking full parental authority, however, most are powerless to help the children work out their relationships, and many fear their stepchildren's power to hurt their younger, adoring half siblings.

"As far as the children go," Mia sighs, "Nick and Amy have been positively cruel to Tracey, who's only four years old. She worships them. Two years ago, Nick bought her a bracelet and she still sleeps with it. Tracey treasures the frayed old toys and weathered books that Amy's given her. Both of my stepkids used to play with her and *seemed* to care about her. But, because of the problems between their parents, they've cut her off entirely. They won't talk to her on the phone, won't answer the letters she painstakingly dictates, won't see her. I understand that they're jealous that she lives with their father when they don't. But Tracey has no idea why they suddenly disappeared from her life. She's confused, crushed. She truly longs for them. We try to explain, but how is a four-year-old supposed to understand?"

Although many of these stepmothers sympathize with their stepchildren's anger, they want to protect their own children from being victimized. Like Mia, some defensively begin to reinforce the separation of their children from their stepchildren and encourage fathers to visit stepchildren alone. These efforts, however, sometimes divide the entire family.

"When Bob came back from his first 'solo' visit," Mia winces, "he positively beamed. He'd had a wonderful visit with Nick. He came home grinning, raised his arms triumphantly in the air and cried, 'I have a *son!*'

"Now, I didn't want to be a party pooper, but I had trouble sharing his happiness. In fact, I felt wounded and separated from him by it. *I* didn't have a son yet, and I didn't expect ever to have one. Was I supposed to be happy that my husband had had one with somebody else? And, since I *did* have a *daughter*, was I supposed to understand that having a *son* was somehow more noteworthy? I doubted that Bob meant to imply that, but there it was. And, since the happy reunion had depended entirely upon Bob's excluding me and our daughter, I didn't exactly share his elation at rediscovering his male offspring. But here's my conflict, my dilemma: I felt I was wrong to cast a shadow on his joy."

Rejected by their stepchildren and protective of their own, these stepmothers face several basic contradictions. They want their husbands and stepchildren to share relationships, but not at the expense of their own families. They want their children to be close to their stepchildren, but not close enough to get hurt by misplaced anger. They want good relationships with their stepchildren, but not enough to fight their intense, continued resistance. Most do not expect that they will ever be able to attain the affection of their stepchildren, unify their families or guarantee that their own children will be safe from emotional harm at the hands of half siblings.

Theirs and, Cautiously, His

Stepchildren who suffer from severe emotional or psychological problems present other difficulties to stepmothers who have their own children. Some are afraid to leave their children alone with their stepchildren because they fear for their children's physical safety. Others worry that relationships with their step- or half siblings may expose their own children to emotional harm.

Jill Sterling is concerned that her suicidal stepson will become a role model for her adoring three-year-old son, Billy. "I don't want my children to be damaged by Charlie's emotional struggles. There seems to be a cloud of pain and mental illness hanging over my stepson, and I'm afraid that my children can get hurt by his depressions if they're around him too much. It helps Charlie to see how Billy adores him. But it doesn't necessarily help Billy to adore someone who's on the verge of suicide."

Although most do not fear that their stepchildren will do bodily harm, many stepmothers are concerned about the negative influence of depression, drugs or delinquency on their impressionable, younger children. Some who have devoted themselves to helping their stepchildren find that their priorities change when they have their own children. Many want to keep their children and stepchildren safely apart, but find that their husbands do not. Like Jill Sterling, they learn that their husbands see all their children simply as siblings, and, as such, encourage close relationships among them.

"Michael wants us to be a totally united family," Jill sighs. "He's happiest when we're all together. He sees things as he *wants* to see them. *He* thinks we're doing fine! He encourages the children to play together, to interact. When Charlie visits, Michael includes our son in almost everything they do. Michael loves all his kids and envisions them staying close all their lives. Playing touch football in the backyard. Or sailing together on the bay. Or living here, under one roof. Michael refuses to let go of his visions, even if our kids could be hurt."

Because their concern for their own children outweighs that for their stepchildren, these women limit the time they spend together or structure the activities they share. Most believe that their own children are too young to fend for themselves and see it as their place, as mothers, to balance the relationships. One describes her efforts this way: "At least until they're old enough to understand their stepsister's problems and to distinguish right from wrong, safe from dangerous, and when and how to say 'no'—until my children can take care of themselves and each other—I'm uneasy about promoting their relationships with my stepchild. What I'm saying is, I won't be comfortable until they're all adults. And, even then . . ."

Theirs and, Maybe, His

While love for their own children leads some stepmothers to distance themselves from their stepchildren, many discover that it brings them closer together. Stepmothers who had "no use whatsoever" for their stepchildren prior to motherhood sometimes find that important relationships develop afterward, usually centered around their own children.

Many of these women, threatened by their husbands' close relationships with their stepchildren, preferred to minimize contact with them. As their own children grow, however, they begin to perceive their stepchildren's roles in the family differently. Those who gave birth later in life are often concerned that their children have "families" that will survive them. Others, who have just one child, want that child to experience sibling relationships. To these women, most of whom have spurned their stepchildren or rued their very existence, motherhood brings new perspectives, and an appreciation of their stepchildren's potential value to their own small children.

Jessie Solomon was forty-two when her son, Adam, now one year old, was born. "When I look ahead, I'm concerned. Mark and I are older parents, so I worry about Adam. I want him to have some family. And so, I'm faced with a major dilemma because, personally, I want nothing to do with Mark's children, Tricia and Todd. I want them out of my little family. But I want *Adam* to have his half siblings. I want him to belong, in case something happens to me or Mark."

Certainly, the feelings these women have about their stepchildren do not change as much their behavior toward them does. They acknowledge the rights of all the half siblings to know and form relationships with each other, but most are motivated solely by their own children's interests. They are willing, they say, to put aside their own preferences and feelings for the sake of their children's future well-being, even if it means opening their doors to their stepchildren.

"I'll manage, for Adam's benefit, to include Mark's other children and their offspring in our family life. Adam clearly needs them more than they need him. Or, he might, someday. And he's my concern. Bottom line is that I love my baby. I'd do anything to make his life more secure, successful or happy, even invite my stepkids to dinner! Well...not *yet*. Maybe in another year, when he's old enough to remember them. Why start before I *have* to?"

Theirs and His Together

Women whose stepchildren live with them have unique experiences in dealing with their own and their stepchildren. Most feel unconditional love for their own children, but say that love has to be earned by their stepchildren. Because "love" in their steprelationships is not automatic, many actually work harder to please their stepchildren than their own. Some try to compensate for their lack of love; others try to overcome it.

Julie Sinclair compares her relationships. "On a daily basis, I probably do more for my stepkids than I do for Emily. This isn't because I have to do more for them; it's because I consider it important. I see our relationships as similar to friendships, built on common interests, respect, participation in each other's lives and on the desire to continue the relationship. Because I'm an adult, I do more of the 'doing' than they do, but I still expect them to reciprocate and to 'do' for me, when they can, what they can. Like friendships, our relationships are subject to evaluation, choice and limits. Consequently, I find myself 'trying' a lot.

"With my *own* daughter, Emily, it's different. I never have to 'try' or 'do' or prove anything. I just *am*. There are no limits, evaluations or choices. We simply *are* mother and daughter. That's unconditional, permanent. I'm hers and she's mine."

These women accept the differences in their feelings for their own and their stepchildren. They do not apologize for these differences and are not ashamed, sorry or guilty about them. One declares, "My feelings simply *are* what they *are*. I try to be responsible and kind to my stepchildren, but I can't force myself to feel love, commitment or devotion."

Julie Sinclair admits, "The 'friendships' I have with my stepchildren are not necessarily permanent. They can end whenever one of us exceeds the limits. One of my limits is lying. My stepson lied to me not long ago and I confronted him about it. I said, 'Without using the words stepmother or stepson, describe our relationship.' He shrugged and said, 'Friends.' I asked him to think about his best friend and what could possibly happen in that friendship to destroy it. He told me, 'He could double-cross me, or talk behind my back or lie to me.' Then I asked him if, as friends, he and I weren't subject to the same sorts of limits. The light bulb went off over his head and he said, 'Yes!' He understands, now, what's at stake if he lies to me again."

Stepchildren are often shocked when they first realize that their relationships with their stepmothers can be lost. Although they understand that their stepmothers are not their mothers, many still seem to expect the same devotion, sacrifice, commitment and unconditional acceptance from stepmothers as they get from their parents. Some stepmothers, like Julie, feel it is important to let their stepchildren know that they must earn acceptance from them, that they must participate, reciprocate and stay within acceptable limits to maintain the friendship.

Despite their open partiality for their own children, most of these stepmothers say that their children and stepchildren get along very well, without excessive jealousy or rivalry. Some attribute their compatibility to the gaps in their ages or to their stepchildren's strong relationships with their own parents. Others give sole credit to their husbands, who love all the children equally and create an atmosphere of unwavering love and acceptance that balances their own conditional relationships.

"When our daughter was born," Julie remembers, "Trevor sat with his other three kids and told them that Emily was the same blood relationship to him that they were, and she'd be a full-fledged member of their family. They apparently accepted that, because they've never seemed to consider her less than their sister.

"Of course, along with the status of 'sister' comes some sibling rivalry. Emily's now at an adorable age and Tori's at a very awkward age, so there's jealousy there, and that gets acted out, like when Tori refuses to lend Emily her old, outgrown toys. And the boys do mischief, hiding the stuffed animal that Emily *must* have if she's going to sleep. Or bribing Emily with candy, to get her to swear that one of them is her 'favorite forever.' But these things happen among siblings, too, not just in stepfamilies. I think they simply consider themselves siblings."

Despite rivalries and occasional resentments, these stepmothers generally consider themselves fortunate that their own children have older half or stepsiblings as role models and mentors. In some cases, the younger children actually bind the family together by creating strong emotional bonds that balance the stepmothers' tentative ones. In others, the little ones break tensions with their honest observations or boost their step- or half siblings' self-esteem by idolizing them, imitating them and craving whatever the older ones possess.

"Emily's never questioned why she has me for her mother while the older three kids have somebody else. She's never asked why the others don't live with their mother. But at dinner one night, she was quietly contemplative and serious for quite a while. Finally, to my dismay, or maybe to my *credit*, she revealed what was puzzling her. 'Mommy,' she asked, 'when will I be old enough to get *my* stepmother?'

"We all laughed. The older kids belted out, *'Never*, you hope!' and things like that. By the time we actually tried to explain things to Emily, she'd lost interest, but she'd also lightened our moods, once again, and made us laugh together. And we felt, in our odd way, closely connected, like a family."

Advice From Stepmothers on Blending Children With Stepchildren

1.   **Don't try to force a relationship between half or stepsiblings.** Just as you can't force a relationship between yourself and your stepchildren, you can't create one among the children. Try to set the same limits for the children as you would for any siblings, and then let the kids find their own common ground within those limits. Expect

that there will be ups and downs, peace and war, love and hate—as there are with all siblings—and try to let them work their relationships out by themselves, with a minimum of interference from you.

2.   **Be aware that *your* children can be vulnerable.** Your children from your present marriage will probably adore the older children. But the older ones are more likely to be, at best, ambivalent. Be aware of the kind of emotional investment your child is making in his stepsiblings and try to evaluate whether or not the investment is safe, wise and mutual. Try to maintain a balance between meddling in the children's affairs and protecting the innocent.

3.   **Don't overcompensate.** Don't do more for your stepchildren to cover up the fact that you might love them less. Don't do less for you own children to hide the fact that you love them more. Don't get caught up in trying to prove to your stepchildren that there are no differences between your feelings for your children and for them. They know the relationships are different; they know how to tell what's honest from what's forced. Just be consistent, fair and open about your interactions with each child.

4.   **Be yourself.** There are no guarantees that your stepchildren will like you *or* your children. They may, but if they don't, don't try to change yourself or your kids to please them. You are who you are. Do what you can for your stepchildren, but if they resist relationships, remember that your primary responsibility is to your own children, your husband and yourself—your nuclear family. Don't neglect your role of wife and mother in the name of being a stepmother.

5.   **Be sensitive to history.** Remember that your stepchildren have been through the separation and divorce of their parents. Their most intimate trusts have been shaken; their foundation of home and family destroyed. They will not welcome a new stepfamily, relate eagerly to new stepsiblings or feel secure about how they'll fit into a new family that arises after the divorce. Children of divorce are deeply wounded; they need special patience and affection.

6.   **Don't expect stepchildren to welcome your new bundle of joy.** Most siblings are, at best, not pleased about the arrival of new babies in the family. Expect this upset to be even more pronounced with the arrival of new stepbabies. Older children, even *adult* children, will be unsure of how the new arrival will affect their relationships with their fathers, or of how it will change their status in

the family. Having already endured the feelings of abandonment that accompanied their parents' divorce, they may well be predisposed to feel and act like outsiders, so try to be inclusive and reassuring to your stepchildren, both prior to your baby's arrival and as soon afterward as possible.

7.   **Remember, it's a two-way street.** The nature of your relationship with your stepchildren is optional, in that both you and they have to agree to it. No matter what your relationship becomes, it is still a mutual creation, and it's a mutual responsibility to maintain it. Don't feel you have to do all the work; stepchildren have to do their share of the communicating and cooperating. But don't expect them to do more than their share. As children, they will probably expect and depend on you, an adult, to do most of the giving. However, although you *are* an adult in your stepchildren's lives, you are not their parent; you shouldn't expect yourself to relate—or to give as tirelessly—as a parent.

8.   **Don't be jealous.** Even if you have no children of your own, try not to feel "left out" of the parent/child bond that your husband and his children share. Realize that this bond is deep but that it doesn't have to take away from what you and your husband have together. It's important to the well-being of the entire family that your husband and his children be encouraged to maintain their bond, even if you are sometimes excluded. If you *do* have children of your own, try not to compare how your husband treats *your* children with how he treats *his*. Try to avoid obvious favoritism, though, and, if it appears, work together to find ways to eliminate it.

EIGHT

The Marriage

The women we interviewed had been married for an average of seven years. The longest of their marriages was nineteen years; the shortest was just under three. As brides, they were typically thirty-one years old. Most described their marriages as "happy" and think that they satisfy their husbands' needs adequately or better. Over three-quarters said that their marriages are successful and secure.

For the majority, the greatest challenges to their marriages are problems surrounding their stepchildren. Some of their marriages have survived these problems only with the help of therapy. The success of other marriages is due primarily to the parental partnerships formed between stepmothers and their husbands. The strains of dealing with their stepchildren have forced an openness and trust in these marriages that might not otherwise have been achieved.

A number of stepmothers believe that their marriages endure because they "compartmentalize" certain family relationships. Some of these women divide themselves into "secret" sides that they keep to themselves and "public" sides that they present to their husbands, families and stepchildren. Others divide their husbands into a "father" and a "husband," so that wife and stepchildren do not compete for the same territory.

Whatever mechanisms they employ, most find that the role of

157

stepmother tests the strengths of their marriages and the bonds between husband and wife. While some confided that their marriages are in trouble and attributed the bulk of their problems to their stepchildren, the majority of the marriages are not only enduring, but have even been enhanced by this testing.

Marriage on a Tightrope

Most fathers and children share histories and bonds that include their own sets of rules and standards and that, intentionally or not, exclude outsiders. Often, the less secure the bonds, the more difficulty fathers and children have in including newcomers.

As newcomers, therefore, stepmothers are expected to remain outsiders and to follow established patterns, rather than to generate new ideas and family relationships. If they intervene, disrupt, question or interfere, they can endanger their relationships with their husbands.

Tensions appear in Jennifer Slade's marriage whenever her stepson, David, visits. "The minute his son appears, Alex's attitude toward me changes. He becomes critical and cold. He mimics the way I talk, complains about my cooking and mocks my expressions. Normally, we're comfortable together, compatible, fond. But when David's there, Alex picks on me, as if, by putting me down, he'll bring David closer. He takes me for granted because he's sure I love him, but he's *not* sure about his son. He puts me down because he wants to show David that he is more important to him than anyone, even me. Besides, Alex is very threatened by David's relationship with his new stepfather. He feels his role as 'father' needs to be protected."

Women like Jennifer end up dreading their stepchildren's visits. Their husbands become so estranged and critical of them when their stepchildren are present that they are forced to compete with their stepchildren for their husbands' attention or affection. But visits are not the only disruptions stepchildren make in these marriages. Some husbands dominate their wives' lives by adhering to rigid and inflexible patterns of communication with their children.

"My stepchildren intrude upon us nightly," one stepmother sighs. "My husband calls them every, and I mean *every*, night, to say 'good night.' At first, I thought this ritual was sweet. But there are no exceptions, no reprieves. No matter where we are or what else is going on, my husband *must* get to a phone between 9:30 and 10:00 P.M. We can be at a dinner party, the theater, the symphony, on a European tour, and, at the appointed time, Chuck has to get to the phone. When I was giving birth to our daughter, he left me in the *delivery room* to call them. I'm serious!"

Most of these women find it impossible to talk with their husbands about their stepchildren, much less about the effect the children have on their marriages. Although they recognize the need to communicate, many believe that confronting their husbands could ultimately cost them their marriage. Some, convinced that the stepchildren are well aware of their own power and influence, timidly avoid provoking their displeasure. Despite outward passivity, however, many stepmothers find that their resentment builds with time and, eventually, affects both their feelings for their husbands and their attitudes toward their marriages.

"The problems with David have begun to spill over onto the rest of our marriage," Jennifer confides. "I don't feel sexually attracted to my husband after these insulting incidents with his son, and the incidents are more and more frequent. It's funny, in a way. At first, after a visit from David I felt ravenously sexual. Sex was one way I could 'reclaim' my husband. It was a way of being close to Alex with which David couldn't compete. But I always felt degraded and unsatisfied afterward because sex wasn't *really* helping me reclaim my status as a respected, equal partner. Nor was it helping us reach new levels of understanding, to prevent more put-downs and mockery. It was merely sex. If anything, it seemed that I was telling Alex it was *okay* to treat me horribly if I made love to him after these episodes. Gradually, I withdrew sexually. I used to be jealous of the affection and loyalty Alex showed David. Now I'm not jealous. I'm angry."

Although most stepmothers insist that they love their husbands, many do not know how long they can endure the exclusions, insults and estrangements that typify their marriages. They hope their marriages will survive until the stepchildren grow up and separate from their fathers. Some say they count the minutes until their stepchildren leave for college. Although disillusioned and bruised, most remain committed to their husbands.

"I still think that Alex and I are basically good together," Jennifer insists. "He just needs to prove he can be a 'father' to David, at any cost. I don't want to be that cost. I want to be his wife. So, I'll keep quiet, pretend to be happy and hold on to what we've got. As long as I can, anyway."

Married to the Judge

Other marriages are in trouble because husbands expect stepmothers to be as deeply involved with their children as *they* are. Unlike those described above who are excluded from parent/child relationships, these women feel that they are pushed into those relationships, only to be judged, graded and evaluated on the interactions that follow. They say that they are "on trial all the time," or that their feelings for their stepchildren are constantly being tested by their husbands. The stress of having to please both their stepchildren and their husbands, often at the expense of their *own* emotions, takes its toll both on these women *and* on their marriages.

Maxine James would not know how to rebuild her marriage, even if her husband were willing to try. "I grieve for the marriage I believed I had, and for the way I used to love my husband. I still *love* Gordon, but not the same way, not nearly the same way... not after all the blame and pressure he's put on me."

The greatest single source of marital strife for these women is their stepchildren. They believe their husbands demand that they love and nurture their stepchildren to excessive, even ridiculous degrees. Some husbands seem driven to prove to their ex-wives how "perfect" their new spouses are. Others are trying to make up to their children for their divorces by providing them with "new and improved" mothers. Whatever their motivations, these men see themselves as the directors of the stepmothers' relationships with their stepchildren, and they become infuriated when their new wives cannot play their roles.

Maxine explains, "It's all about what Gordon wants me to feel about, give to and do for Tina. I do a lot for my stepdaughter but I get blame for not doing more. Gordon seems to interpret my limitations as a lack of love for *him*. His attitude is, 'If you love me, you have to love my kid.' But *I'd* like to ask *him*, if he loves *me*, why he can't understand me and my feelings? We're at a complete deadlock."

Communication has broken down in marriages like Maxine's. Many of the husbands flatly refuse to discuss problems and dismiss any suggestion that the couple should seek counseling. The women see their marriages as cycles of increasing and decreasing tensions that center around their stepchildren's visits, during which they feel they must prove their love, usually by granting the stepchildren their every wish. Opposing, disciplining or limiting them in any way incurs the wrath of their husbands. With time, many stepmothers get tired of placating manipulative stepchildren and appeasing judgmental husbands. Some begin to assert their *own* wills, even though they're aware of the dire consequences.

When Maxine recently refused to buy her stepdaughter an expensive outfit, Tina had a major temper tantrum, which Gordon supported. As the visit drew to a close, Maxine dreaded being alone with Gordon. "I was consumed by tension," she says. "After Tina left, Gordon and I circled each other, like caged tigers waiting to pounce. We couldn't, and can't, communicate. We can't share. We can't empathize. We can't *hear* each other. We aren't really a couple anymore. There are no small disagreements. *Any* time I fall short of his expectations there's a colossal fight."

For women like Maxine, their stepchildren are not the problem; their marriages are. Even when their stepchildren are absent, problems and tensions remain. Some believe that their husbands irrationally, often unconsciously, want to punish them for not being their stepchildren's "real" mothers; others believe that their marriages have disintegrated into power struggles in which their husbands try to dominate them, using the stepchildren as mechanisms of control.

Although some have begun to assert themselves with their husbands, most women in this situation have little hope that their marriages will improve. Some have had their self-images so damaged by their husbands' reactions to them that they have independently sought counseling. Most believe, like Maxine, that their marriages would benefit from therapy, but know that their husbands would never participate.

"Gordon won't *consider* outside help. He's too independent and proud to admit he has a problem. Besides, he's convinced that the problems are all mine."

Secrets Brides Veil

Some stepmothers hide their true feelings about their stepchildren from their husbands because they believe revealing them would hurt their husbands and their marriages.

"There's no point in Mark and me discussing his children," Jessie Solomon explains. "There's nothing to be done. They exist. Mark can't do anything to change that, nor can he stop caring about them. And I can't expect him to banish them from his life. Short of an extreme like that, there isn't much that would satisfy me, because it isn't the *particular* stepchildren that bother me. It's the fact that there *are* stepchildren."

These women describe themselves as "idealists" or "romantics." They see their husbands as "soul mates" and male "counterparts" whom they are unwilling to share, even with their stepchildren. They describe their marriages as "pure romances," except when their stepchildren intrude.

Despite their claims of perfect love and romance, women like Jessie hide many of their feelings from their husbands and shut out a large part of their husbands' lives. When they realize that, regardless of adulthood and physical distance, their stepchildren remain permanent family members, they become jealous, possessive, insincere, insecure. Some find excuses not to participate in their stepchildren's visits; others create occasions on which they can manage and control contact between their stepchildren and husbands.

"Mark knows that I postponed marrying him because of his children," Jessie says, "so he's sensitive to my feelings about them. He already tries to minimize contact between us. But, now that they're adults, I'm sure he believes that I've come to terms with his children, that I'm no longer tortured by their presence. And that's how I want it. I want to spare Mark any further conflict about this issue, even if I have to lie and disguise the truth. Because there's simply no sense bothering him about something he can't change."

Another stepmother says, "My stepchildren represent our separateness. No matter how close we become, how much we share, or even how many children we have *together*, my stepchildren are a living wedge, dividing our lives."

These women are not proud of their feelings. They reveal them cautiously and are often ashamed, embarrassed or saddened to do so. Some call themselves immature, selfish or hypocritical, but they steadfastly refuse to reveal their real feelings to their husbands. Although their secrets mar what they see as otherwise flawless marriages, few seem to realize that their secrets compound the divisions between them and their husbands and add stress and anxiety to their lives.

"My secret," Jessie confides, "my inability to tolerate Mark's children, is the single but constant source of pain for me in our marriage. There is nothing I, or Mark, or even his children can do about it. It's just there, all the time. And it will probably give me an ulcer."

Marriage by Compartments

Other women carefully conceal their feelings for their stepchildren from their husbands for different reasons. Many believe that the stability of their marriages depends on keeping their warm, positive relationships with their stepchildren out of their husbands' sight. They see their husbands as extremely possessive of the stepchildren, competitive for their affection and jealous of anyone who comes close.

These stepmothers refuse to submit passively to their husbands' wishes. Instead of relinquishing control and permitting their husbands to define their relationships with their stepchildren, they take charge subtly, through direct communication with their stepchildren outside their husbands' spheres. They describe their families as "subdivided" or "compartmentalized" and separate their own relationships from their husbands', allowing their husbands their own territory.

"When I tried to be part of the relationship between Keith and Brittany," Jamie Simpkins recalls, "I was frustrated, jealous and angry at my husband. It was only after I stopped trying that I was able to cope. I was even able to find some peace in my marriage."

Occasionally, issues regarding their stepchildren's discipline, limits or finances arise, reminding these stepmothers of the delicate balance in which their marriages hang. Convinced that their husbands will oppose *any* position they take regarding these issues, many avoid discussing them altogether, in order to prevent arguments.

"The truth is that I'm irritated with my husband," Jamie admits. "It annoys me that we can't talk about Brittany. The fact that, after all these years, he still needs an exclusive attachment to her puts me off. We get along much better now that we've stopped discussing her. But having a taboo subject, *any* subject, in our marriage is a sign of a weak spot."

Overall, women in situations like Jamie's find that the key to survival in their marriages lies in letting go of the part of their husbands that "belongs" to their stepchildren. They divide their husbands into internal segments designated to one or another family member. Most do not conduct this division passively; they also remove parts of themselves from their marriages, in order to establish their own exclusive relationships with their stepchildren.

Jamie explains: "I've come to accept that Keith's relationship with his daughter is *his* business, not mine. I watch, notice and have opinions, but I leave it to them. I view their relationship as outside the domain of my marriage. In fact, I think of Keith as two people: my husband and Brittany's father. I don't expect the same things from Brit's dad as I do from my husband, and I can clarify my expectations if I mentally divide him this way."

These women are convinced that their marriages can succeed if they continue to separate and structure their steprelationships. Most are deeply in love with their husbands and say that their marriages are well worth the effort. However, they admit that their marriages are not what they had hoped they would be, and that they resent the limitations their husbands impose on them.

"Meantime, I treasure the compartment I share with Keith. I try not to expect more from him than he can deliver and I do whatever I can to make our marriage comfortable for us both. Keith is worth it. I love him. And, there's enough love in Keith for all of us. It's just a shame he doesn't know that, that he thinks he has to divide his love and, by doing so, his family. But we'll take him, whatever way we can."

Married to a Silent Stranger

Some marriages are generally secure and happy, except that the husbands' personalities change whenever their stepchildren are around. Many normally outgoing husbands become tense, withdrawn, nervous or quiet. Some men feel overly pressured to "make" everyone get along. Others are afraid to do or say anything "wrong" in front of their visiting children. Whatever the reasons, these husbands behave differently enough to upset their wives and, sometimes, their marriages.

"Bob became a silent stranger whenever his children visited," Mia Jordan remembers. "He didn't know how to please *all* of us, an so he just click-whirr-buzzed out. He was present physically, but I'd often have to say something to him two or three times before he'd respond. It was like being married to a zombie. He was so careful about what he said and did that, to be safe, he said and did *nothing.*"

Women like Mia do not know what to expect from their husbands when their stepchildren are present. Although they realize that the purpose of the visits is to give their husbands and stepchildren time together, most say that the burden of the visits lies with *them* because their husbands seem unable to participate or communicate, let alone orchestrate activities.

"I end up carrying conversations," says one stepmother, "and trying to move the whole group along toward something resembling 'fun,' while this tall, handsome, semiconscious shell of my husband stumbles along with us. I'm exaggerating, but not much. He isn't himself."

Many find that the marriages are affected by their husbands' passive, silent behavior. Some watch their husbands change instantly from strong, self-reliant and aggressive to vulnerable, frightened and powerless. Others describe their husbands as "defeated," "anticipating rejection" and "torn between pleasing their children and establishing new lives for themselves."

Overall, these women have mixed reactions when they confront these new sides of their husbands. "First, I felt protective, almost maternal," Mia recalls. "I wanted to shield Bob from anything that could hurt him, even from his children, and so I tried to speak and act *for* him, and tried to energize our visits. But, eventually, I stopped because it did no good. *I* could not replace their father. They wanted to hear from *him*, not *me*.

"But also, I felt something more insidious. I felt angry at Bob for losing control of his relationship with his children. I saw him as weak, in that he hadn't been able to secure his own children's respect and loyalty. I felt a primitive uneasiness, as if I didn't know if Bob were capable of fighting to protect his own interests. And that made me angry, because I needed to feel that I could rely on him, that he could protect me and our children. I resented these doubts. I hadn't imagined that my stepchildren would shake my marriage so profoundly."

Some of these women try to take charge of their marriages when their stepchildren are around, leading their husbands into positions that imply leadership and strength, such as athletics or competitive games. Others, concerned that their stepchildren might interpret their father's silence as indifference, try to demonstrate that their mute husbands are nevertheless caring and devoted.

Many find that their husbands' awkwardness eventually spreads to them. Like their husbands, they begin to feel self-conscious around their stepchildren, especially about expressing affection. Some begin to feel that their stepchildren observe them, searching for signs of marital discord. Under these watchful eyes, some stepmothers force demonstrations of spousal affection to make it clear that their husbands' withdrawn attitudes do not reflect problems in their marriages.

"Oh, let's talk about affection," one stepmother says. "If my husband as much as puts his arm around me or kisses me when his kids are around, they involuntarily wince or shudder. You can almost *feel* their revulsion. Intimacy between us so clearly bothers them that I try to avoid *any* expressions of love during their visits. My husband, however, seems to need to hug and touch, even to cling to me, more than usual, and I find myself pushing him away. When he touches me, I can feel my stepchildren's eyes searing my skin."

Mia says that her husband became distant during her stepchildren's visits because he felt torn between two roles that seemed mutually exclusive: her husband and their father. She understood his withdrawal, but it bothered her enough that she occasionally asserted the existence and strength of their marriage.

"I remember once wanting to hold Bob's hand in some mall where we'd taken his kids. I actually wrestled with myself about whether or not it was *okay* for me to do that when my stepkids were with us. Finally, I decided it was all right. So, daringly, in clear view of his children, I took his hand. I decided that it was good for them, once in a while, to see that we do, actually, hold hands, that we are a couple. And so we walked, hand in hand, but I couldn't relax or enjoy it. It was a deliberate, self-conscious act, one that I did simply because I wanted to prove I *could*."

The sex lives of some of these women simply disappear when their stepchildren visit. Their husbands retreat, and they feel uncomfortable expressing love, even in the privacy of their bedrooms.

"My husband I rarely even touch during their visits," one confides. "Even when my stepchildren are in bed, asleep, it's like they're with us in our room because they're so heavily on my husband's mind. He's so preoccupied and I'm so inhibited that we simply don't make love when they're in the house."

Among these women are some who say that their husbands' behavior changes are primarily due to continuous battles with their ex-wives. For a few, like Mia's husband, these battles escalate to the point where visits stop altogether. Even when the stepchildren are not physically present, however, these husbands are affected by the pain of separation and the frustration of endless conflict.

"Bob's past marriage hangs over us like a dark shadow," Mia says. "His ex-wife is committed to revenge, and she's poisoned my stepchildren's minds against us. Bob tries to hide his sadness regarding Nick and Amy. But, in doing so, he shuts off part of himself from our marriage. And no matter how hard he tries to protect me, we, as a couple, are bruised by his children. We feel their absence the same way you'd notice two empty chairs at dinner, or two empty beds at night. Perhaps it's a sign of how close he and I have become, that we feel the grief together. Neither of us is immune to the other's pain."

Despite the problems that emerge when their husbands "change," these marriages are generally stable and successful. Most of them have ultimately benefited from what the stepmothers have learned about their husbands. Although they may not *like* everything they have learned, they certainly have achieved more accurate, realistic images of their spouses, which allow them to form stronger bonds.

"Bob and I love each other deeply," Mia says. "Because of my stepchildren, I've learned about how he deals with loss and frustration, just as he's found out about my limits for seeing him and our family hurt. I'm convinced that what we've learned has helped us. We know each other thoroughly, not superficially. We accept each other as imperfect, as human, and we try to help each other where we know the other is vulnerable. It hasn't been easy, but it's been worth it."

Married to a Yes-Man

Some husbands lose the ability to say "no" whenever the stepchildren are around. "He becomes a wimp," Marla Jenson says. "A total marshmallow. A spineless blob. Revolting."

Marla says she loves her husband and is happily married. In fact, she considers her marriage ideal, except where her stepchildren are concerned. Most women in similar situations believe that their husbands feel guilty about their divorces and that the ex-wives encourage the stepchildren to play upon this guilt, particularly by emptying their fathers' wallets.

"If Steve found it easier to communicate with his children, our marriage would be better. He can't. He wants to say, 'I love you,' but he doesn't. He says, 'You want it? I'll buy it for you,' even though he can't afford it and they don't need it. It's a pattern. They pull his string, he dances. They've created havoc with my marriage. They've drained our bank accounts and determined which house we live in, what vacations we do or do not take and what car I drive. We feel tremendous pressure to earn enough money to cover all their rents, tuitions and other fees."

Many women admit that their husbands' unwarranted generosity to their stepchildren has affected their spousal relationships. When they see their husbands repeatedly submitting to outrageous demands, many stepmothers lose respect for them. Others find that their reactions are more basic.

"When I saw my stepkids kick sand in my he-man's face, and when I saw him *let* them dance all over him, two things happened," Marla says. "I got angry and I got turned off. The man that my stepchildren play like a puppet is not the man I'm attracted to, *not* the man I thought I'd married. It's not that I use sex as a weapon. It's that I found it difficult, at least during the first few years, to see Steve act so passive and then go to bed and think of him as my counterpart. I'm strong and I need a strong partner. Suffice it to say that our sex life suffered when I thought Steve was so weak he couldn't even stand up to his own kids."

Some of these women find that their respect for and attraction to their husbands drops so low that their marriages are endangered. Although they realize that they can neither allay their husbands' guilts nor stop their stepchildren's demands, few are willing to remain passive while their financial and emotional resources are drained. In order to save their marriages, they find compromises that work for them, often putting lids on what their husbands spend on the stepchildren.

"I cope by setting limits for my stepchildren in our home and by setting aside money in a 'matching gift program' for our daughter and me," Marla explains. "The effect this has had on our marriage is to make Steve aware that I will not be part of his guilt trip about his kids, even if I understand it. He knows that I can only be pushed so far, and then I push back. So he tries to communicate more and spend less. And, the more he tries, the less angry I am. As I've grown to accept that Steve just isn't *Steve* where my stepchildren are concerned, my attraction to him has stabilized. I just divide him, mentally, into my husband, their father and her ex-husband, and I see those as three separate guys. It may sound crazy, but it keeps our sex life alive."

In order to save their marriages, some of these women bully or terrorize their husbands more fiercely than their stepchildren do. They are convinced that their husbands cannot tolerate conflict and will obey whoever poses the greatest threat. Others simply want to create a much needed balance to their stepchildren's enormous influence. Most agree that their strategies have made their marriages stronger, if not wiser.

Marriage Under Thunderclouds

Some stepchildren have needed so much attention that stepmothers and their husbands have had little opportunity to pay attention to their marriages.

"He's affected my marriage, all right," Jill Sterling laughs. "My stepson *is* my marriage! It seems that Michael and I have never been without him. Whether he's actually visiting or not, Charlie is always on our minds. It's been that way from the beginning."

Most women who, like Jill, have stepchildren with serious emotional or physical problems, plan their daily lives, activities, work schedules and marriages around their stepchildren's needs.

"In the course of dealing with Charlie's problems," Jill says, "a 'friendship,' of sorts, was forged between me and Michael's ex-wife, Ellen; one that I'd never have sought out, otherwise. Knowing her has affected my marriage, because I see my husband, now, through the eyes of the woman who divorced him. And that's certainly not improved my image of him."

These women were usually completely unprepared for the crises their marriages brought them. As newlyweds, they suddenly confronted their stepchildren's drug addiction, teenage pregnancies, serious illnesses, car accidents and suicide attempts.

"What I'm saying," Jill explains, "is that my marriage has required me to spend the bulk of my energy and emotion not on my *husband*, but on his son and ex-wife. Our lives are centered on Charlie. Controlled by Charlie. How is he? Has he talked about death today? Does he seem any better? Is he eating? Doing his homework? Talking to friends? We're on constant alert and I'm in continuous communication with Ellen."

Another woman, whose stepchild has been diagnosed as schizophrenic, remembers that it took years before she realized that she was unhappy, or even that her marriage was not typical. "My husband and I *never* have time just for ourselves. At first, I didn't mind because I was so happy to be married to him and didn't realize how serious things were, how long it would last or how much she'd demand of us. We're coming up on our sixth anniversary, and we've never taken a vacation. My husband won't leave in case something happens to my stepdaughter while we're away."

These women have learned more about their husbands by how they relate to others in the family than by how they relate to them. Through crises, each has discovered how her husband reacts under stress, how he deals with frustration and how vulnerable he is when his children are threatened. As wives, many have felt as if they were drowning in the needs of their husbands' former families. Some have had to fight to keep their husbands, and their marriages, afloat.

Sometimes, their emotionally disturbed stepchildren make stepmothers uncomfortable about being intimate or even affectionate with their husbands. As wives, they become inhibited, self-conscious and sometimes frightened. "My twelve-year-old stepson spies on us," one woman declares. "He watches us, whatever we do. When my husband and I think the kids are asleep, we sometimes close our door and make love. After awhile, if I get up to get a snack, I often find my stepson standing outside our room, claiming to be 'on the way to the bathroom.' One night, I woke up to find him standing at the foot of our bed, staring at us. We have no privacy when he's around. I don't think he's dangerous, but he scares me when he appears from nowhere, silently watching us."

Despite the stress of these problems, most of these marriages are successful. Often, family therapy has helped them survive. Whether through therapy or through the learning that results from shared traumatic experience, most of these stepmothers believe their marriages are improving. Ironically, many claim that their husbands would never have become as sensitive, or learned to communicate so well, were it not for their stepchildren's problems. Overall, they are surprised that their marriages do so well, given that the spouses have so little time to devote to each other. And they share a common desire for more "normal" lives.

"I don't think Michael has any idea," Jill confides, "how deeply I crave some time, just a week or two, for us to be a carefree couple, or even the relatively carefree parents of two small children. I don't think it would occur to him that we might, sometime, want to focus just on ourselves and our own two kids, without worrying about Charlie all the time. How delicious that would be."

Marriage as a Package Deal

Some stepmothers feel married not only to their husbands, but to their stepchildren, their husbands' ex-wives and all their related problems, as well. Most say that their husbands appreciate their efforts as wives and stepmothers, but that they lack an understanding of how demanding these roles are.

"Even with all the appreciation he expresses," Maggie Joyner says, "I don't think my husband's ever considered how his son has affected our marriage. Brad just accepts him as a given, a part of *our* family. He assumes I accept him that way, too.

"But I don't, not quite. Because Josh is not just part of *our* family; he's also what keeps Brad's former marriage alive. Josh is the child of Brad's ex-wife and he keeps their relationship active. So I am always aware that I am Brad's 'second wife.'"

Like Maggie, many stepmothers feel that their marriages are "second-hand." One explains, "Nothing is *new*, for us. I was my husband's second bride, at his second wedding. We went on his second honeymoon and I had his second child. Whatever we do, it seems overshadowed by his past."

Others do not see themselves as necessarily second best, but they agree that their husbands' pasts dominate their marriages. "It's not that I'm jealous of the past marriage," Maggie explains. "I'm jealous of the *present*. I can't help feeling that *my* time, *my* marriage to Brad, *our* family keeps being invaded by the past. I get upset when Brad says things like, 'When Josh was born, we got puppies.' *We* didn't get puppies when Josh was born. *I* wasn't even in the same state as they were. The perpetual 'we' excludes me. It refers to the former family, the first family, and it damages our marriage, or how I feel about our marriage. Or how I think Brad feels about our marriage. It's as though nothing we do is new or quite as romantic because it all happened *after* another romance."

Some complain that their stepchildren keep their parents so closely involved that it seems that these parents are still, somehow, married. "Sometimes," one woman remarks, "I feel like we're all married to each other, with no boundaries or privacy. I feel like my husband and his ex aren't divorced, but that he's merely taken an additional wife. And I feel this way, even though I get a lot of thank-yous from my husband for putting up with his kids and former wife, and even though I know I have his trust, confidence, affection and complete commitment."

Even with the problems, most stepmothers find that their step-children have provided cause for their marriages to deepen and grow. They are convinced that, without stepchildren, they would never have known their husbands as well or, certainly, have seen their vul-nerabilities so clearly. They are sure that as stepmothers they have won their husbands' complete trust, in ways that they would not have been able to as mere wives.

"My husband relies on me as if I were an extension of himself," one comments. "No, actually, he trusts me *more* than he would trust himself."

For many stepmothers, marital success depends on their ability to reshape their responses to their stepchildren. What they used to see as intrusions by their stepchildren, they redefine as their husbands' inclusion of them in the most intimate and important parts of their lives. What they originally perceived as competition from their husbands' former wives, they redefine as nuisances from which they can protect their husbands. Most come to believe that their husbands respect them as stepmothers, and that their gratitude and trust have enhanced their marriages. Their experiences with their stepchildren have proved to them that their marriages can endure the worst kinds of stress and that they can weather anything, even their *own* weaknesses and shortcomings.

"The way our marriage has been affected by my stepson has been a mixed bag," Maggie sighs. "But when you're committed to someone enough to marry him, you take the whole package, and you work with it to make it be the *best* you can. I think we've done that."

Mutual Admiration Society

For some women, being stepmothers has only a slight, but positive impact on their marriages. They see their marriages as "romantic" and view stepmothering as just another vehicle with which to demonstrate their commitment to their husbands.

Molly Jerome elaborates. "I simply insist that everything between Ed and me be an expression of our love. And that includes being a stepmother to his children. And, because I see my stepmother role as mirroring my other bonds with Ed, my course of action is always clear. I'm Ed's spokesperson. Or his helper. Or his public relations officer."

Like Molly, many of these women feel like representatives or even extensions of their husbands, especially where their stepchildren are concerned. Some find themselves defending their husbands against accusations made by the stepchildren's mothers. Others are constantly explaining their husbands' behavior to their stepchildren, to minimize conflicts and soothe friction between fathers and children. Many find that their stepchildren misunderstand their husbands, and take it upon themselves to step in as middlemen.

Molly says, "I'm always reminding them, 'You have to hear your dad's side of the story before you make up your minds,' because my stepsons always get angry with Ed about stuff that never even *occurs* to him. My stepsons don't understand their father, so it's my job to remind them that they need to try to get to know him. They take him for granted, so I try to give them some perspective."

The more these women share with their husbands, the closer they grow and the more solid their marriages become. In helping their husbands' relationships with their children, they feel more bonded to and more appreciated by their husbands.

"It's not always easy," Molly admits. "I try to show the boys the image of their father that *I* see and love, to counter the image their mother presents. Where she tries to convince them he doesn't care about them, I consistently point out his expressions of affection. When I think I've swayed them even a little, I feel glorious. I really do. So our marriage requires that I be much more than a wife. I'm also a fanclub president, PR spokesperson and cheerleader. It's a lot," Molly shrugs, "but it comes with the territory."

Married to the Whole Kaboodle

Women whose stepchildren live with them describe a unique set of effects that these "permanent residents" have on their marriages.

Julie Sinclair learned that her husband's children were to live with them only weeks before her wedding. "My stepchildren have made me a better wife," she declares, "at least on a day-to-day basis. 'Better' in the sense of more responsible. The fact is that my husband doesn't have time to do much around the house, even though he does what he can. So, the cooking, cleaning, laundry, ironing—all those awful things that I'd have preferred to avoid doing, fall to me. If not for my stepkids, I'd probably let the laundry pile up until we ran out of underwear, and I wouldn't dust or vacuum unless we were having company. The fact is that the earliest impact the kids had on our marriage was that I became a good housekeeper."

These women see the daily care and maintenance of their step-children as fundamental to their marriages. Some were not prepared when they married to have their stepchildren live with them and had to make big adjustments to accommodate them. Many found that their privacy disappeared, that they had little time alone with their husbands and that even their sex lives changed when their stepchildren moved in.

"Once, when we were newlyweds," one recalls, "my stepkids got up early and hid under our bed, to surprise us in the morning. We didn't hear them. I don't know how they managed to stay so quiet. Maybe they fell asleep, but we had no idea they were there. At any rate, when we woke up, we didn't hear any stifled giggles or notice any movement under the bed. We were busy on *top* of the bed. It wasn't until we lay back, cozily about to doze off again that we heard laughter and saw a hand come up from under the bed. A second later, there were these two innocent little kids giggling and jumping on our bed, asking us what all the bouncing had been about.... My stepchildren were always, *always* there, always intruding.

"Now that they're bigger, our private times read like the TV Guide. If a local team is playing on prime time, we know we'll be able to have two hours alone that night. But I don't think we've *ever* made love on a Tuesday night, because the kids don't like anything on TV on Tuesdays. It's kind of a pain in the neck, but it's not really a problem. It's just one very noticeable way they affect our marriage."

Privacy, responsibility and their sex lives are not the only aspects of marriage affected by the presence of stepchildren. These women say that their impressions of and feelings for their husbands often change. A few are disappointed that their husbands delegate so much parental authority and responsibility to them. Some are disillusioned because they think do not provide a strong paternal model. However, the great majority find that their stepchildren have improved their marriages by enhancing their images of their husbands.

Julie remarks, "I have endless regard for the sensitive way Trevor deals with being the *father* of my stepchildren. Especially when we were first married, Trevor was our anchor. He was the person who had to bring all the pieces together and do it in some way that could mean 'happiness' or 'family,' for us all. He was happy that we were married and delighted that his children were going to live with us. But he had to make those two, quite independent, sources of joy mesh, despite the odds."

Women like Julie see their husbands as ringmasters in the circus, orchestrating the competing and often conflicting needs of everyone in the family. "Sometimes, the kids being happy meant I couldn't be," Julie says. "And sometimes the opposite was true. But, somehow, Trevor always made either outcome seem okay. He compensated for any unhappiness.

"For example, one Saturday, soon after our wedding, I wanted Trevor to come pick out new wallpaper for our bedroom. But Kevin had a Little League game that day, so I went to look at the wallpaper myself. Trevor went to the game. I was angry all afternoon. The issue wasn't the wallpaper. It was how badly I needed to do something, anything, alone with him. When I got home, Trevor presented me with a box of chocolate marshmallows, my favorite, and told me he'd hired a babysitter so he could take me out to dinner. My anger melted away, and I realized that never, not for a moment, had he forgotten about what I needed. No matter what the issue or the other demands on his attention, he always thinks of me."

Although many mourn the time and energy they spend on their stepchildren, most of these stepmothers do not feel that this is at the expense of their marriages. Instead, they say that their stepchildren have helped unite them and their husbands as couples and that their husbands' talent for attending to everyone's needs leads them to love them even more deeply. If not for their stepchildren, many doubt that they would have had the opportunity to see the depth of their husbands' generosity and sensitivity.

Julie's stepchildren gave her marriage a focus, from day one. "Because of my stepchildren, we were never able to go through the usual adjustments newlyweds go through. We didn't have a chance to live under the newlywed 'microscope' where each examines the other and their 'coupleness.' Instead, we had to focus on raising children. We had to be a team, on the lookout for the kids to play one of us against the other, forced to develop parenting strategies. In that process, we talked about values, morals, philosophies—things we'd never have analyzed or shared as quickly, or ever, on our own."

Overall, their stepchildren's presence in their homes gives these women and their husbands clear views of each other. Most like what they see, and believe that their stepchildren add to their marriages. Whether or not they enjoy the *process* of being custodial stepmothers they agree that the *role* enhances their growth as wives and as individuals. In raising their stepchildren, they and their husbands go through a lot together and grow as a couple. Their marriages, most agree, can only be better for that.

Marriages in Jeopardy

Some of the women we interviewed do not appear in this chapter because they have already sought or obtained divorces for reasons directly related to their stepchildren. They explained that they could not endure their husbands' behavior around their stepchildren, their stepchildren's attitudes toward them, the roles delegated to them within the stepfamily or the overall effects the stepchildren had on their marriages.

Among the survivors, about a tenth say their marriages are in jeopardy, largely because of their stepchildren. And although most of the rest claim to have happy, successful marriages, over a third have, at some point, sought marital or family therapy; two-thirds say that their images of their husbands have been damaged; and about three-quarters say that their sex lives have been adversely affected because of their stepchildren.

Despite these problems, most stepmothers say that having stepchildren has deepened their commitment to and understanding of their husbands. Most believe that they have matured and grown as individuals, and that their marriages have been strengthened because of their stepchildren. Although there are floundering marriages, their numbers seem far lower than the national norms, which find a third to a half of all marriages ending in divorce. If, as our small sampling appears to indicate, the marriages of stepmothers are more sturdy than average, it may be because the very nature of their marriages is different.

As brides, stepmothers tend to be older and presumably more mature, experienced and responsible than most. But it is not only the bride who is different; the nature of the commitment she makes is different too. Even as these brides say, "I do," they are aware that they instantly obtain stepchildren. They commit not just to a man, but to his children, as well. The weight of that commitment makes most of them think very carefully about their marriages *before* they enter into them. Even if they do not even remotely suspect the specifics or the extent to which their marriages and lives will be affected, they know that their stepchildren will figure heavily, somehow. Unlike some new brides, these women anticipate that their marriages will be challenging and, thus, are not likely to back out of them at the first, second or even third crisis.

Advice From Stepmothers on Marriage

1.   **Put your marriage first.** Do what you have to do to get your marriage where *you* want it. Be willing to compromise everything but your marriage. If your marriage can't please the entire family accept that, even if it requires the exclusion of some family members. Accept the facts as they are, take care of your marriage and be happy.

2.   **Be on your husband's team.** Solidarity between spouses is of utmost importance. Don't let your stepchildren or their mother or any of their issues come between you and your husband, if you can help it. Make your husband see you as his strongest ally where his kids are concerned. Make him feel comfortable about talking to you about them. Help him. Treat your stepchildren as you would any other aspect of your husband's life; pitch in and be his partner, and make sure the

kids *see* you as his partner. As much as you can, share your husband's goals for his children, and let him know that you share them by helping him achieve them.

3.   **Communicate.** Be honest with your husband. Let him know your feelings and limits, and then act accordingly, so no one will be surprised or disappointed. Be open and candid, but let him know he can count on you to support his needs regarding his children, even if your feelings are in conflict. He needs to know you'll do your best and that you are united. But he also needs to know your true feelings, whatever they are, so that you don't begin a pattern of withholding from each other. If there are issues to be resolved, talk about them honestly. But if there is nothing that can be done, or if you think your husband simply can't deal with the issues, consider whether talking will help or hurt your marriage. Sometimes it may be better to keep the stark truth of your feelings to yourself.

4.   **Keep smiling.** Talking isn't the only way to solve problems. Provide positive energy, affection, humor and a sense of fun. Happiness is contagious. Remember that marriages and families connect people. Everyone touches everyone else. If you happily help your husband, he'll appreciate you, he'll feel happy and his happiness will touch the children. And the children will reflect their dad's good mood, or at least be influenced by it. And that will come back to you. It's a big circular, ripple effect, and whatever you toss into the pool—playfulness or love or sorrow or anger—will spread.

Always consider yourself a role model, even when you think nobody's watching. Show your husband the way you want things to be. Show his children the example of how a marriage *can* be. Live by setting examples.

5.   **Don't expect perfection.** You and your husband will probably *never* be in perfect harmony, especially where his children are concerned. See your relationship as a process, rather than a constant. If you look at a marriage as a way of growing together with someone, a way of sharing life together, your relationship will flow more easily from day to day. Accept the need for constant adjustment. You may have perfect moments, but each day brings new challenges and new needs for adjustments.

6.   **Be prepared for disruptions.** Be prepared *not* to have your husband's full, focused time and attention. His children may take as

much of him as they can get, and he may never feel that he's giving them enough. Be prepared to have constant interruptions from his kids, his ex-wife and her entire extended family, especially when major events occur, like birthdays or holidays or chicken pox or school plays—for all occasions, all vacations, every weekend for the rest of their childhoods. Be prepared to have uninterrupted time with your husband rarely, if ever.

7.   **Consider your options, including professional help.** Secrets are part of life. Secrets that help your sense of self, or that help you feel good, are fine. But if, as wife and stepmother, you find yourself overburdened by your secrets, if you have to hide your "true" self to sustain your marriage, you need to talk to somebody, maybe somebody other than your husband. Let the secrets out. Breathe. Counseling might help.

8.   **Let your husband have his own emotions.** Don't expect your husband to understand your feelings about his children. He may have enough trouble dealing with his *own* feelings and conflicts concerning them. And he probably has a completely different view of them than you do. Where his kids are concerned, you and he will probably always have different perspectives. You are separate individuals; you do not share common histories or relationships with his children. When you can, let his feelings prevail. Assume that his needs, about his kids, are greater than yours.

9.   **Set limits.** Limit your role to what you can live with. If it goes beyond that, get help. Don't undervalue yourself. Don't live in fear of speaking up. If you feel like an intruder in your own home, or if you feel you just can't please your husband no matter what you do, or if there is some other pattern in your marriage that makes you feel you just can't cope: Get Help.

NINE

The Fall of the Wicked Stepmother

As little girls dreaming of their futures, not one of the women we interviewed had fantasized about becoming a stepmother. Even those who had *had* stepmothers never imagined that they would step into that role one day. To the contrary, many decided that under no circumstances would they ever participate in another stepfamily. Although our sample was neither large nor random, our findings suggest that nobody aspires to become a stepmother. No one spends years honing skills and preparing appropriate techniques. The role is filled by women who happen to marry men who are fathers, not by women who want stepchildren.

It follows, therefore, that most new stepmothers are thoroughly unprepared for the role. They generally start out with high goals and good intentions, but few have any real idea of what being a stepmother encompasses. Most start out with altruistic, vague plans of "fixing," "assisting" and "loving" their stepfamilies through whatever difficulties ail them. At the very least, they intend to develop caring relationships with their stepchildren and to become integral parts of their husbands' families. Soon after their weddings, however, most are sorely disappointed with both their accomplishments and their roles.

The Matter of Success

Much of their disappointment stems from the lack of success stepmothers feel in their roles. Although stepmothers define success in a variety of ways, most agree that it is elusive. Some see success in terms of rewards, but feel that their rewards are greatly outweighed by their losses. About a third, in fact, find no rewards whatever in stepmothering. Those who *do* find rewards describe them as mostly intangible, including deepened relationships with their husbands and increased self-knowledge.

Stepmothers' losses, however, cover a far wider range: feelings of personal failure and powerlessness in relationships, drained finances, deferred pregnancies, impaired marriages and damaged self-images.

Other stepmothers measure success not in terms of what they gain from their experiences, but by how they meet the needs of other family members. Almost three-quarters say that, as stepmothers, they meet their husbands' needs well; over half meet their stepchildren's. Only a third, however, meet their *own* needs; the rest do not.

Finally, a number of stepmothers mark success according to enjoyment of their roles. Measured by this standard, most claim failure. Only a quarter genuinely like their roles, while half actively dislike them. Dissatisfaction with the role of stepmother is clearly widespread.

Dissatisfaction and Disappointment

Many find their dissatisfaction overwhelming. Some of the women we interviewed became so distraught by their experiences as stepmothers that they divorced their husbands prior to the completion of this book. Others feel that their marriages are barely surviving, delicately balanced on the issue of stepchildren. Almost half are actively unhappy about being stepmothers and over half admit that, given another chance, they would probably choose *not* to accept the role.

Even though they are initially unprepared, it still seems incredible that so many competent women become thoroughly stymied by their roles as stepmothers. These are not, after all, the malevolent witches of folklore and fairy tales. These are successful, mature women, well-liked, well-educated, well-motivated and well-intentioned. What *is* it about the role of stepmother that makes success so difficult for so many women in so many different circumstances?

Although there is no single, simple answer to that question, we believe that, most of the time, the root of the difficulty lies in the assumptions and expectations stepmothers themselves bring to their roles.

Expectations, Ideals, and Goals

Most stepmothers enter their roles with at least a few unreasonably high expectations. For example, many expect themselves to change, help or improve others. They expect to have strong, positive relationships with their stepchildren, creating "happy" or "loving" stepfamilies. They expect that their husbands will support them in their efforts as stepmothers and behave consistently in their separate roles as husbands and divorced fathers. They expect that their stepchildren's mothers will be cooperative, motivated by their children's best interests, and basically neutral toward *them*. And they expect that their stepchildren will be curious, perhaps even eager, to get to know them. Unfortunately, most of these expectations are unrealistic, even naive. All of them require the combined efforts of others in their stepfamilies and are, therefore, beyond the scope of the stepmothers' control.

There are, however, other reasons that their goals are unrealistic. Those who expect to "fix" their stepfamilies forget that they were not present when the problems began and are, therefore, not a party to them. As newcomers, it is unlikely that they can grasp the impact of experiences they did not share, much less be able to find solutions to the problems these experiences may have created. Further, it is unknown whether their help would even be welcome.

Impractical goals based on preconceived notions of stepfamilies are a common source of stepmothers' disappointments. Other disappointments often result from naive expectations of others. Many stepmothers mistakenly assume that their husbands, whom they saw as strong, rational, supportive and understanding in other areas, will act strong with their ex-wives, rational about their children, or understanding and supportive of them as stepmothers. The majority discover that their husbands are of little or no help to them, since, as fathers, they are too conflicted, insecure or unsure of their *own* postdivorce relationships to function effectively, let alone to be supportive of somebody else.

Many women also err in their expectations of their stepchildren. Frequently, they do not fully comprehend the emotional impact of divorce and its aftermath on children. Before stepchildren can be interested in knowing, much less *welcoming*, their stepmothers, they have to work through their reactions to their parents' separation and the loss of their nuclear families. Most of the time, stepmothers come into their stepchildren's lives before that healing has been completed.

Further, unlike mothers, who *choose* to have children, who share parenthood with their husbands, and who bond with their babies all through pregnancy, birth and infancy, stepmothers are usually presented with fully developed children, whose births they have neither planned nor necessarily desired. The stepmother role often requires that they nurture and care immediately, before they can establish *any* attachment or bond. For many, the pressure to "mother" on demand breeds an unanticipated resentment that is very difficult to deal with, deepens and eventually affects the entire stepfamily.

Another commonly mistaken notion of stepmothers is that their stepchildren's parents will encourage their relationships with their stepchildren. Many are surprised to learn that their stepchildren's negative attitudes toward them are enhanced by their parents. Particularly if the parent with physical custody, whether father or mother, opposes the stepmother, her stepchildren are likely to reject her. And, regardless of *who* has physical custody, if the *mother* opposes the stepmother, the stepchildren are likely to reject her, as well. Many find it impossible to establish ties with their stepchildren because of mothers who, overtly or tacitly, deliberately or accidentally, block their efforts. Other mothers intrude upon their children's relationships with stepmothers by becoming high-profile members of the stepmothers' inner circles, insisting that their title of "mother" entitles them to permanent places in the step- or blended families. Those women who expect their stepchildren's mothers to remain neutral and quietly accept them are often, at the very least, disappointed.

When they realize that their expectations are unreasonable and their roles more complicated than they anticipated, most stepmothers are dismayed to find few, if any, role models and little literature to assist them. Even families and friends provide scant emotional support, understanding or guidance. Stepmothers, in fact, are often embarrassed to confide in others, assuming (or assuming that *others* will assume) that it is their "fault" if they have problems with their stepchildren. Some believe that their situations are unique and doubt that anyone, particularly anyone who is not a stepmother, would understand, much less be able to offer useable advice.

New Goals and Roles

Fortunately, there *are* some ways that stepmothers can improve their chances for survival, even for satisfaction.

First, they have to replace unrealistic, idealistic expectations with well-defined, attainable goals. More important, they must give themselves both the power and the permission to define, as well as to enjoy, their *own*, if limited, successes.

Until they define "success" based on their own goals, stepmothers stand little chance of achieving it.

However, before they even *begin* to define success, stepmothers must acquaint themselves with the individuals in their stepfamilies, their histories, the relationships among them and the dynamics through which they interact. Within this complicated context, stepmothers must identify both how they *can* and how they *want* to fit in, and whether there is any overlap between the two. If, and *only* if, there is a match between the role that a stepmother *selects* and the one that her stepfamily can *accept*, does she have a chance for success of any kind.

Tools and Rules

Once stepmothers have studied their stepfamilies, determined the roles and responsibilities they want to take on and defined success, there are several important tools they can use. The single most important and powerful of these tools is *communication*.

In marriages where stepmothers and their husbands communicate well, issues regarding stepchildren tend to fall in place with all the other issues they discuss and manage together. Where there is a breakdown in communication, however, issues related to stepchildren tend to take on more than ordinary significance and become symbols of other problems in the marriages.

Where stepmothers and their husbands stand together, share ideas, reveal feelings and support each other's goals, their marriages can survive almost anything, including stepchildren. Problems and emotions are addressed together, compromises are reached, balances achieved. Even tough problems, in the context of firm commitment and open communication, became manageable or, at the very least, tolerable.

Marital survival, however, is not necessarily synonymous with a stepmother's "success." Even many who communicate openly with their husbands and feel successful as wives admit that, as stepmothers, they feel like dismal failures. Although this sense of failure is, most often, related to self-imposed, unrealistic definitions of success, many say that even *after* they assertively modify their goals, improve their communication and define their relationships, success in and enjoyment of their roles remains elusive. By its very nature, they claim, the role of stepmother is forever challenging, changing and just plain tough.

Stepmothers often encounter situations that would present problems in *any* family, without having clear ideas of where they personally fit into the problem *or* the family. In our interviews, *every* stepmother of teenagers reports that her stepchildren have had *some* trouble with drugs, liquor or other "delinquent" behavior. For others, major unpredictable crises arise due to changes in careers, job locations, finances, physical custody or child support. The birth of a new baby creates a host of new problems. Many are in a constant spin because, no matter *what* they do, the ever-changing developmental stages of stepchildren continually reshape the nature and intensity of their relationships. Further, the role does not necessarily get easier with time—challenges often grow with stepchildren, and college, weddings and step-grandchildren promise that the list of issues to grapple with will never end.

No stepmothers, it seems, are immune, regardless of the strength of their marriages or the level of their communication skills. However, as they come to realize that they themselves must manage their roles, some begin to acquire mechanisms that help them deal with all the issues, crises and passing phases they encounter. They accept that they can neither change nor satisfy others *all* the time. They try to discover their own limits of patience, availability, cheerfulness and flexibility, and to learn how much they can give honestly, sincerely and without resentment. Ultimately, they learn that they do their best as stepmothers only when they give top priority to their marriages and their *own* happiness.

The Voice Within

Overall, it is impossible to define a universally "successful" stepmother. The word "stepmother" is, after all, just a word, meaningless apart from a specific person in the context of specific relationships. A successful stepmother, therefore, can be no more and no less than a woman who has done her best within the parameters she has chosen for herself. To succeed, she must define her own relationships and try to realize them. If, however, her stepchildren do not reciprocate, she has not necessarily failed. She may feel hurt, but if she has sincerely done her best, she is still "successful."

Stepmothers should not expect their roles to be easy. Nor should they relinquish responsibility for their decisions to marry men with children. They *should*, however, hunger for understanding, emotional support and acknowledgment of their efforts by their husbands, their stepchildren and society at large. Support groups for stepmothers, literature presenting practical information or even a national holiday honoring stepparents might meet some needs. But, more than any of these external acknowledgments, what stepmothers need is to acknowledge *themselves*. They need to recognize that they have sole control over their roles and that it is not only their prerogative, but also their responsibility to make their *own* decisions. In setting their *own* limits and priorities, there will certainly be no lack of issues for them to tackle. Achieving open communication, defining their goals and limits, and strengthening their marriages are good places to start.

Tomorrow's Families

Daily, over a thousand brides become stepmothers to almost twice as many stepchildren. Certainly, the challenges of restructuring the American family are not exclusive to stepmothers. Stepchildren, fathers and mothers each have their own sets of related problems and conflicts. As their numbers grow, however, stepfamilies are becoming increasingly dependent on stepmothers' abilities to deal with their own roles. The longer these women feel isolated or powerless, the longer it will be until they are able to contribute either to their stepchildren's development or to their families' well-being. We hope that the day will come soon that when people hear the word "stepmother," they will not think of the evil woman in *Cinderella*, but of sensitive, positive women who contribute significantly to the quality of American family life.